SUPERSTITION AND THE
SUPERSTITIOUS

SUPERSTITION AND THE SUPERSTITIOUS

ERIC MAPLE

SOUTH BRUNSWICK
NEW YORK: A. S. BARNES AND COMPANY

SUPERSTITION AND THE SUPERSTITIOUS. © 1971 by Eric Maple. First American edition published 1972 by A. S. Barnes and Co., Inc., Cranbury, New Jersey 08512.

Library of Congress Catalogue Card Number: 71-124212

ISBN 0-498-07431-5
Printed in the United States of America

To Judi

CONTENTS

LIST OF ILLUSTRATIONS

PREFACE

WITHOUT EXCEPTION all of us will have been conscious at some period in our lives of an uncanny sense of insecurity. The world around becomes threatening, certainties dissolve into uncertainties—suddenly we become afraid. This is not necessarily an irrational attitude : it is often our moment of truth. Only then are we face to face with what some people might call reality, a truth so overwhelming that it seems to threaten sanity itself. It is at this time that we turn away from the world we know to those secret powers or spirits which our ancestors believed waited at the side of every individual under duress to see him through the crisis. We perform little secret rites that we feel may somehow counter the blows of fate, or at least offset imaginary disasters. These rituals which are probably as old as humanity itself, we call superstitions, but to an earlier generation they were known as magic.

The nature of mind still defies analysis, but behaviour has become the fascinated study of our psychologists, who have noted among the many curious facets of human activity a constant deference to secret rules in daily life. Even the avowed atheist will act in a crisis as if there really existed a supernatural power. Consciously or unconsciously, all of us when in dire extremity attempt to control the external environment by particular conscious physical and mental actions. Superstition does not merely consist of the avoidance of ladders, or the throwing of pinches of salt over the left shoulder, or even joining some group in which occultism is practised on a collective basis. Expressed in simple terms, superstitions indicate an acceptance of the existence of powers that are superior to humanity and which can be made to submit to the human will. It is a common illusion that people are far more superstitious today than in the past and it is said in support of this contention that mankind, in despair at the failure of its new deity, science, has returned to the older fetishes which were discarded when the first rosy promise of a man-made heaven began to cast its treacherous glow on the horizon. This perhaps does not really explain the vagaries of the human mind.

In the opinion of the author there is no reason to suppose that the mind of man has changed at all within measurable time and that, therefore, our behaviour in situations of crisis can be regarded as an unvarying expression of a common inheritance, an implanted pattern.

Without doubt, however, the focal point of superstitious belief has varied from age to age. Not so long ago we concentrated the whole of our superstitious feelings within a religious framework, as at an even earlier period of history we accepted wtih equal piety the laws of magic. Today, in an age of declining religious faith, more and more people are openly turning to magic. Gone at last is the old reticence. In terms of occultism we are now a permissive society and the field is clear for an open avowal of superstitious beliefs which, in a more prejudiced age, would have been concealed from the outside world.

Perhaps man never really changes and at heart is destined to remain forever the aspiring magician, his eyes blinded by the vision of a world of wish-fulfilment in which either the wand or the will are employed to thrust back into the outer darkness from whence they came the demons of despair.

In presenting this survey of contemporary superstitious beliefs I have found my greatest obstacle in the inability of most individuals to recognise their own superstitions, yet at the same time, while disclaiming any superstitions of their own, many are adepts in recognising those of others. In the main they tend to regard their own beliefs, not as superstitions, but as facts of life. An incredible number of people unquestionably accept the existence of second sight and ghosts and will rarely concede the possibility that they could be victims of some illusion.

I had anticipated at the outset of this venture that I might bring to light a vast treasure of new superstition superimposed upon the crumbling strata of the old. What in fact became manifest was that most of the old superstition had still survived intact, and that even when a new superstition was discovered it proved to be no more than an updated version of an old one. I do claim, however, to have resurrected many unsuspected superstitions from among all strata of the population. Children, I found, were the least inhibited of all my subjects, a veritable treasure house of an ancient lore which must have been handed down from the remote past. If any really significant fact has been established as the result of this survey it is perhaps that the world of the child could well be the reservoir from which humanity draws most of its psychic beliefs, and that in their twilight world of magic we may see the microcosm of our adult psychic selves.

CHAPTER I

ORIGINS

THE ORIGINS of our superstitions are lost in time and those beliefs which have survived are often relics of ancient cultures and long vanished ways of life. Above all, however, they remain outward expressions of the tensions and anxieties that rend humanity as it struggles down the corridor of life from birth to death, buffeted by the alien winds of chance. Life, now as in the past, remains an impenetrable mystery with incomprehensible rules, and the vast majority of individuals implicitly accept the existence of an external power which in some mysterious way influences their lives and which it is believed can sometimes in an equally inexplicable manner be influenced by the human will.

Such a power has been given a variety of names, including good and evil, god and devil and even white and black magic. To most of us, however, it is summed up by the single word luck. Luck is the unknown goddess, perhaps the first deity ever to have been conceived by primitive man, and possibly, when the last pantheon of the gods has crumbled to the dust, she will remain the single survivor of the ages of faith.

It is around this inexplicable term luck that all our superstitions revolve, in attempts to capture its mysterious power and convert it temporarily to human use. Unlike fate, however, luck, if all the sages of the ages are to be believed, is capricious and fickle and must be wooed in order to be won. In many ways it is like a woman; it is "Lady Luck". The techniques mankind employs to lure this elusive creature into the human net have descended to us from the ages of magic under the name of Superstition.

The word superstition is derived from the Latin words *super* : above, and *stare* : to stand. In ancient times those who survived in battle were called *superstites* because they had outlived their fellows. Our modern superstitions fall into this class for they so often represent apparently bizarre modes of thought that have survived the ages which created them, to linger on in our midst like ghosts from an unknown past.

It was in this sense that our ancestors used the term superstition when they condemned the religious dogmas of their opponents. The Romanists regarded pagan beliefs as superstitions, while to the Protestant Reformers the beliefs of the Roman Catholics were mere "popish superstitions"; and our modern humanists are often ready to brand *all* religious beliefs as superstitions. Generally speaking, however, the term is used to describe forms of belief which are no longer regarded as valid, whether they consist of eccentric medical theories or faith in outmoded religious dogmas or certain stylised idiosyncracies of behaviour. The term superstition, however, should not properly be applied to wrong-headedness or illogicality unless these conditions happen to be based upon concepts of a mystical kind. Basically superstition and all that it involves is concerned with specific attitudes towards the world of spirits.

At the root of most of our surviving superstition lies an implicit acceptance of magic as a rule of life, which in effect means the possibility of control by man over his destiny by the exercise of key actions—rituals—to which the forces governing the external world have no option but to submit. It would therefore appear that the superstitious individual basically regards the animating forces behind nature as possessing quasi-human qualities, despite the fact that they belong to a different order of creation. Like the scientist the magician of old sought to force the submission of nature to the human will; unlike the former, however, he believed matter to embody elemental spirits, and not elements, and these he wooed, coerced and commanded by the use of special words or by specific actions, like the waving of a wand. The world of the magician is a domain of conflicting forces represented by hostile and friendly spirits, and to win the favour of the latter without antagonising the former is his primary task.

Today we, like the magician of old, constantly seek to come to terms with these forces of good and evil which, expressed in day-to-day terms, are called good and bad luck. To win over the good spirits and keep at bay the bad, however, far more is needed than willpower alone. In its struggle to maintain self confidence in face of the hostile winds of disaster, mankind has preserved only what has been absolutely essential to its survival. Included in this precious heritage are our superstitions, those ritual acts of faith which were specifically designed to offset the destructive influence of fear and to provide for man an imaginary control over the environment which gives the race confidence to struggle onwards towards its destiny.

The extent to which perfectly rational people will turn to magic
in their daily lives is not generally realised. Often the most level-
headed individuals place a considerable degree of faith in a lucky
charm or some similar object which they half believe will afford a
degree of protection against misfortunes in general. At times of crisis
the whole situation may become dramatised with the charm being
secretly rubbed or held tightly in the hand to draw on its power as if
it were the source of a store of energy.

The principal interest in a lucky charm is provided by its historical aspect, for in its design it reflects the religious beliefs of antiquity
rather than the latter-day magic of the twentieth century. Lucky
charms in general fall into two main categories: the personal
good-luck bringer, which is usually carried in secret and is rarely
discussed because of the fear that by so doing one diminishes its
strength; and the more general charm which was originally devised
as an amulet for the aversion of misfortune, and which, like the
medallion of the saints, is usually openly displayed, as if to outstare
any hostile force in the vicinity. An ordinary charm bracelet can be
an object of fascinating study if the various charms are considered
individually, for they represent some intriguing aspects of the
magical lore that has been handed down to us from the remote past.
An extremely interesting example is the lucky pig mascot which was
carried in medieval times to protect a peasant's home and family,
and particularly his domestic pig, from the malice of witches and
the evil eye, despite the fact that such pagan observances must have
been highly objectionable to the medieval church. The secret of the
charm pig's magic lies in the fact that it is the symbol of the Sun
Boar which in ancient Scandinavia was a divine animal possessing
great psychic power. What was more natural than that the peasant
of old should have placed his domestic pig under the protection of
so powerful an animal as a sacred pig, not to mention his wife who
was probably nearly as valuable to him as his farm animals.

The power of forgotten religious faiths to influence the superstitions of later ages is responsible for that other inseparable embel-
lishment of the charm bracelet, the horseshoe, which in its general
shape represents the crescent moon and derives its protective power
from the fact that Moon worship was once an integral part of the
religious life of ancient Egypt; that great culture was the traditional
home of magic and the original source of many of our beliefs in this
field. The iron horseshoe is particularly potent for the additional
reason that the first specimens of this metal discovered by man fell

upon the earth in the form of meteorites, and naturally enough was thought to have been a sacred element bestowed upon man by the sky gods.

The cat, another permanent member of that charmed circle of the charm bracelet, was (as is well known) sacred to the Egyptians and was not only worshipped but treated with a loving care that it was not to know for a further 2000 years, during which period of time it went into eclipse as a luck-bringer, becoming instead closely associated with black magic.

An entirely different principle applies in the case of the elephant charm or the elephant hair ring which some people consider to be very powerful magically. These objects represent the strength of the animal itself, and in effect bring to the wearer a superior physical power to resist misfortune or to achieve a desired objective. In savage society, wearing the teeth of a tiger or the claws of a leopard as an amulet enhances the power to resist evil and thus serves similar ends.

The lucky rabbit's foot charm, an old favourite although sadly in eclipse today in urban society, is typical of a class of magic based on the totem animal. In Ancient Britain the fox, the cat and the hare were totemic beasts sacred to the inhabitants, and the foot or tail of any of these would have provided for its owner the protection of the animal he worshipped. The history of the rabbit's foot charm provides one of those rare examples of the evolution of a modern superstition from a primitive religious rite. The hare was a sacred animal up until the advent of Christianity, a fact commented upon by Julius Caesar. With the advent of the new faith, however, pagan practices became outlawed, and if they survived at all it must have been in the form of minor observances to which the Church was unlikely to take strong exception. So the worship of the hare was replaced by the superstitious practice of carrying one of its feet in pocket or purse as an additional insurance against evil in case the new god should fail to live up to expectations. With the coming of the Normans in 1066, however, the rabbit was introduced to the British Isles and in course of time the superstition became transferred to this animal which so resembles the hare.

Among the somewhat eccentric objects which are carried for magical protection are stones with holes in them, and sometimes flint arrowheads, which have usually been passed down the family from earlier generations. These are typical rural amulets and although far less common today than formerly they deserve mention if only for the fact that they have a clearly defined history extending back to remote times. In the past, when no conception of the primitive aboriginal inhabitants of these islands existed, it was automatically assumed that artefacts of this character must have been made by the fairy race or primitive dwarfs as at that time no other explanation appeared possible. For this reason the arrowheads were given the name "elf bolts" or "elf shots", and it was assumed that they must have been fired from the sky upon mankind below. Elf bolts were held to be responsible for most of the diseases of farm animals and men, and it was for this reason that they were adopted as charms, being thus compelled to defend the very objects which they were designed to destroy. Holed stones served a somewhat similar purpose when hung in stables, for they protected the horses from witchcraft, and in bedrooms they provided psychic defence against nightmares. Finally they ended their days as magical amulets in the waistcoat pockets of the twentieth century countryman.

New objects have always had a powerful magic of their own, but the modern housewife who keeps a newly-minted coin in her purse as a luck-bringer would most certainly be amazed to learn that she is subscribing to one of the most ancient magical practices in history and one which is closely bound up with an outmoded attitude towards agriculture. Because of their instinctive fear of novelty or change, primitive communities the world over have always regarded the first occurrence or recurrence of any phenomena as evidence of the working of the supernatural, and for the barren earth in spring-time suddenly to bear fruit must have seemed to their eyes almost a miracle. The first appearance of the new crop was therefore made the occasion for a great deal of feasting accompanied by ceremonial magic and at such a time a wish was considered to have a greater likelihood of fulfilment than at any other. By analogy the wishing process was extended even further to include other "first things"— the New Moon for example and the making of resolutions at the New Year. The housewife who keeps a newly-minted coin as a lucky charm in her purse is therefore unknowingly subscribing to the belief in the magic of new things, for she makes a fetish of the first of a new crop of coins which to her mind provides not only a magical guarantee that her purse will never be empty but also gives psychic protection against the possibility of its loss.

Any object can be utilised as a lucky charm, but in the main only those that have acquired and maintained their reputations as luck-bringers are likely to come into general use. The will to believe is, however, a most powerful factor in life and there are occasions when a likely object can acquire a reputation as a charm almost over-night; as for example when a lecturer friend of the author gave a talk to women at a luncheon club on the subject of cowrie shells, upon which she is an authority and afterwards distributed a number of specimens, at the same time informing her audience that in the South Seas cowries were regarded as luck-bringers. On returning to the same audience some time later she was amazed to discover from some of those who had attended the original lecture that since receiving the shells their fortunes had changed decisively for the better. In this instance the potency of the charm was apparently derived from a single remark.

A brief survey of the lucky charm industry of today clearly indicates that it is the traditional charms that remain the most popular. Shopkeepers report that the best-selling lines are always black cats, horseshoes, rabbits' feet and white heather. There are, however, some surprising newcomers to this field, as at Whitby, Yorkshire, where a shopkeeper discovered to his amazement that a demand for minute glass ducks was a direct result of the reputation they had acquired in the locality as bingo winners. Irish leprechauns and Cornish piskies will always find a ready market, particularly the latter which, together with its Devonian counterpart, the pixie, once formed an integral element in the minor mythology of the British Isles. Joan the Wad and Jack o'Lantern, which are the male and female aspects of Ignis Fatuus, or fire spirit of the Fens, are lucky charms also widely distributed.

The development of the magic charm industry has gained con-siderably from the ever-widening interest in the occult which is a feature of our own times. Small cuttings from the "Wishing Cork Tree" are dispatched from Devon to the four quarters of the globe, this particular charm being indirectly linked to the sacred cork oak of mythology which was worshipped in classical antiquity.

Integral to magic and superstition is the power of touch. In witchcraft, for example, once an object has been in contact with another a mystical relationship between the two has been established that can never be broken. In mythology we read of the Golden Touch, in psychic healing there is healing by touch, and now in the middle of the twentieth century a touchstone charm is on offer as a tranquilliser. Faith, fantastic faith, once wedded fast to some dear fiction, hugs it to the last. The tactile factor in the human approach is possibly an integral part of our natures. It is apparent that many perfectly rational individuals find a great deal of pleasure in touching reverently some object from the past, possibly because this gives them the sense of having established contact with their ancestors of long ago.

One is constantly amazed at the survival of so many of the more ancient types of magical belief in the form of superstitions, and one wonders how it can be that a scientifically orientated community should cling so tenaciously to symbols representing religious systems that have largely vanished from the world. Every one of our charms has survived centuries of religious change, and often persecution, for the old Church did not look over-kindly on relics of the pagan past. One can only assume, therefore, that they were left alone because they satisfied a human need and, this being so, they are likely to be with us for many centuries to come.

Superstitions being of the idiom of the people, are taken in with the mother's milk, so to speak, and become integrated with the language of thought. Yet it would appear that there is a further channel of communication, albeit an ill-explored one, consisting of the community of children itself, for there is no doubt whatsoever that the child lives in a psychic world of its own, preserving beliefs and customs that have survived almost intact from the early history of the human race. The attitude of the child towards its magic is in the main direct and uncomplicated : above all the child, unlike the adult, is unashamed of its fetishes. A brief study of childhood attitudes to superstition might therefore be useful in widening our understanding of the role played by the occult in later life.

Children, of course, live in a remarkable world where thoughts are things and to many, especially the younger ones, magical ideas play an immense role in the life of playground and school. As with adults the lucky charm is the most common form of symbol in general use and is resorted to on occasions of stress like school examinations, and of course on the sports field where it is not uncommon for both teams to march as to battle under the protection of some gigantic teddy bear or similar totem.

Most of the lucky charms in common use by children despite being representative of an older strata of belief, tend in the main to be unstylised spontaneous creations arising out of some special need or circumstance. A brief survey of a few of the charms used by school-children in the author's own locality produced an amazing array of metal owls, china dolls and a surprising number of snap-shots of domestic animals and horses which emphasised the tradi-tional role of the animal as a luck-bringer. Among other favourites were holed stones and lumps of coal, the most ancient types of luck-bringer in the British Isles. A common feature of the more individual type of charm was the fact that it had usually been received as a present from a loved one.

With children as with adults an object acquires its initial author-ity as a luck-bringer by reputation, and a really effective charm will often pass from hand to hand by exchange or may even be purchased. Yet, with a pleasing directness, a child is more immedi-ately aware of the failings of his charm and equally more ready to admit to the fact than any adult, and should it not live up to its reputation the charm will soon be discarded—but, of course, replaced. It is significant, however, that the exhausted or discredited charm is rarely thrown away, doubtless out of superstitious rever-ence for its past services as a talisman, and is instead usually relegated to some out-of-the-way corner of a drawer or it might be passed on to another person. "I was given a lucky snake," a boy told the writer, "but after it rained every day of my holiday I gave it away to another boy." Likewise a St. Christopher medallion which failed to do its work was rapidly demoted and now languishes in a desk, unloved and unseen. On the other hand, by a kind of inverse logic, a child who failed an examination on the very day she had forgotten to bring her lucky-cat mascot with her to school, decided that this constituted absolute proof that the mascot really had luck-bringing qualities and as a result she kept two lucky cats in her purse from that time forth.

With children also there are special rules that have to be observed if the charm is to function properly, and some of the rites are carried forward into later life. An animal charm must stand upright facing its owner, thus propelling the luck in his direction, and not away from him as would be the case if its position were reversed : whilst an elephant charm must always face the door, standing like a sentry ready to repel all hostile invasions from outside.

An ill-explored area of childhood beliefs is represented by what may be described as love magic which is practised by girls of thirteen years and onwards, the lucky charm in such cases being a special dress or article of jewellery. The principles behind love magic are extremely interesting. In the words of one young devout believer in latter-day pagan rites : "If the first time you wear a dress you win a new boy friend the dress is a lucky one, and you always wear it again when you want to win another boy, but should you lose a boy friend the first time you wear the dress it becomes an unlucky one—a 'jinx'—and so you don't risk wearing it again." In the same way a pair of earrings rapidly went out of favour once the young owner had associated the wearing of them with a subsequent run of ill-luck in love.

Fear of presuming upon the future is another well entrenched superstition common to young and old alike. A little girl explained her method of offsetting disappointment by what she imagined to be a purely personal system of mental magic. "If I say to myself I am *not* looking forward to a party this makes it absolutely certain that the party will be a good one and I always enjoy it."

Thus the charm verbal and otherwise derives its magical power by association of ideas and in this way the lore of the modern school-child displays a close kinship with the lore of savages and with the culture of our barbaric ancestors of long ago; yet this in itself invites the question in the mind of every investigator into this field of research : What is the main channel of communication for the superstitions of everyday life? Almost certainly, to use a term which has been made familiar by the title of a famous work in this particular field, the major medium of transmission is the lore and language of school-children,* which is passed on from one child to another or transmitted from the mother to the child of each generation, thus linking young and old in an unbroken psychic chain extending backwards in time perhaps to the dawn of human development.

* *The Lore and Language of Schoolchildren,* Iona and Peter Opie (Oxford 1959).

CHAPTER II

HOUSE AND GARDEN

THE HOUSE is traditionally the centre of family security, a shrine protected by its roof and walls from the elements and by its door from the invasion of the unwanted intruder, but it is in many respects a psychic centre, having a profound influence upon the emotional life of its inmates. This aspect of a household life is, of course, not unknown to the great majority of home-lovers but it is only when the premises are invaded by burglars or threatened with demolition that some of that older and deeper attachment comes to the fore.

During all the ages of its development from the cave dwelling or the rude structure in the trees to the modern urban villa the house has accreted to itself a host of superstitions and customs most of which are immeasurably old, and the reasons for which are little understood by the men and women of today.

The term "spirit of the home" is a familiar one but there was once a time when the domestic scene was supposed to be under the auspices of a very real spirit whose personality pervaded the household and who in later ages became the inspiration for the common belief in lucky or unlucky influences in the home. Possibly the last relic of this older stratum of superstition is that held by prospective house buyers that a particular house has either a welcoming or a hostile atmosphere, and this is often a deciding factor in the purchase or rejection of a particular property.

Reference has been made to the security given to a household by its door, which in ancient times was supposed to be the means of ingress not only of the stranger but also of invisible spirits from outside. It is for this reason that some of the older doorways are set beneath the carved head of a cherub (originally it would have been a powerful deity), and for this same reason the superstition still persists that it is unlucky to enter a new home for the first time by the back door, as this entrance is not protected by the gods against hostile spirits. A very well-known form of door defence against this type of danger is, of course, the iron horseshoe. However, if it is to serve for protective purposes alone the shoe should be suspended with the convex side upwards. As a luck-attracting charm, however, the horns should point upwards so that the luck is unable to "run out".

The implicit acceptance of the existence of spirit forces threatening a home is no doubt responsible for the superstition still common among women, particularly in the north of England, to the effect that an unlucky "presence" who enters the home may be withstood and often overcome by developing a state of fearlessness through meditation. In the past, before the current housing shortage rendered it virtually impossible, a superstitious householder who sensed an evil spirit would probably have moved elsewhere without delay.

Since the house is regarded as a centre of psychic force it is understandable that many tenants should continue to show a marked aversion to the number thirteen as a house-number, for this is ill-omened and closely associated with the fate of the unlucky thirteenth guest at the Last Supper, and with the death by violence of the thirteenth god in other cosmologies; and its use therefore threatens the security of the dwelling place. Other time-honoured rituals which are still observed in connection with the house entrance are similarly rooted in the theme of the sacred threshold. Thus, when visiting a house, it is essential to leave by the same entrance as one enters it and should one for any reason have to interrupt the journey and return to the house, it is necessary to sit down and count ten—or count seven backwards—before resuming it. It is also very important that a departing guest should not be watched out of sight, as this means he will never re-visit the household.

It would appear that the ancient magic of the threshold continues to influence in a subtle way our thought processes in many unsuspected directions. No doubt the vast majority of those who observe these minor idolatries will laugh at themselves for their foolishness, but the real point at issue is that the rites continue to be honoured in a perfectly serious manner.

Where the open fire still survives it provides a focal point for a body of superstitions that are rooted in the most remote antiquity, for fire was once regarded as the sacred flame of the gods and tended with infinite care like a holy altar. The hearth was the home of the Roman domestic sprite, the Penate, and later the

Cold iron in the form of a pair of scissors, when placed under the door-mat, is supposed to keep off misfortune and witchcraft.

Ever since Roman times, a gift of flowers has been a luck-bringer.

Universally, to sweep outwards from the door sweeps away your luck.

A modern obsession—avoid treading on the lines of the pavement if you would escape bad luck.

medieval house-fairy or Hob, and even now something of the old legendary lore continues to influence nuances of behaviour in the form of superstitions. One of the most persistent of these is the rule that one should never poke another man's fire until one has known him for at least seven years. The original reason for this belief was that it supposedly took that long to integrate a stranger into the corporate body of a family, and that for a comparative newcomer to lay a hand upon the domestic shrine offered open insult to the Hob. And why seven years, it may be asked? The insistence upon this particular length of time is related to the old anatomical belief that one's whole physical body underwent a complete change every seven years, at the end of which time one became in effect a completely new person. Therefore, only after this probationary period had elapsed could a stranger be integrated into the family and be permitted the privilege of poking the household fire.

Fire-lighting superstitions still survive wherever an open fire exists and there will invariably be someone to step forward with that old wives' tale that, if a fire refuses to draw, the poker must be placed crosswise against the bars. Few of us would recognise this as an ancient device to offset the powers of darkness, the hereditary enemies of fire, by forming a cross, the symbol which no evil spirit, witch or demon dare defy. Even more curious is the belief that a fire cannot be lit if it is in the direct path of a sunray, and this relates to the old belief that the first human flame was stolen from the sun, and that the greater luminary is still jealous of puny attempts of the presumptuous inferior flame to emulate his celestial power. That there are many who are prepared to insist that these hearth rites have a scientific foundation is evidence of the degree to which we are all prisoners of the past.

The very strong superstition that it is somehow unlucky to pass another on the stairs which is held by a vast number of normally unsuperstitious people, is the direct heir to the ancient conviction that stairways and ladders symbolise the means of ascension to the abodes of the gods, as in Jacob's dream in the Bible, and there is reason to believe that it is the old awe of treading on the same stairways as a god with the possibility of incurring his wrath which is responsible for the present superstition. Those who inadvertently find themselves in this situation, however, can always protect themselves by crossing the fingers and thus call upon the protective powers of Christ or, if they are sufficiently pagan, by touching wood possibly because at one time in our history trees were worshipped as deities and to touch the sacred wood was supposed to supply protection against all evil.

As to house furnishings, these still inspire some strange emotions among the more superstitious of householders. A clock that stops without warning is considered to be a sign of forthcoming death, as also when it strikes thirteen. This common domestic superstition has its roots in the primitive attitude to life which regarded the personality of an individual as integral with his possessions, the one reacting upon the other. Thus the stopping of the clock indicated cessation of the life of its owner. Almost all clock-striking superstitions were originally associated with our earliest timepiece, the church bell.

Most individuals are inclined to suffer a faint pang of apprehension upon breaking a mirror, believing that in some mysterious way they have condemned themselves to seven years' bad luck. In this superstition we see one of the oldest principles of reasoning at work, for to our ancestors as with many primitive peoples today one's reflection in water or glass was another "self" or soul, and to damage the image automatically harmed the original. For this reason any disturbance of the reflection constituted a threat to one's good fortune and health, and the seven years it required for the ill luck to run out, was based upon the same principle as that described in the superstition of poking the fire of a friend. However, there are a number of antidotes to bad luck of this kind, all of a magical character. In the north of England, for example, it is customary to wash the broken pieces of glass in a south-running stream, as this washes away the bad luck, or to bury them in the earth, which neutralises the evil. In Ireland a mirror that apparently breaks of its own accord is always taken out of the house at once, as is one that falls to the floor undamaged for no apparent reason. The mirror superstition is still in a state of evolution and will often take novel forms. A very recent development is a nervous fear of damaging the protective silvering in a thermos flask, for which the only remedy is to wash the container under the water tap. There are a great many variants of the broken mirror theme and all relate to the fate of the soul. Mirrors are covered at the time of death in the household, lest the reflected soul of the deceased should carry off one of the mourners to keep it company on its last journey into the vale of darkness and there is of course the odd belief that an uncovered mirror surface attracts lightning. Many people insist that even to look into a cracked mirror is highly dangerous, since this causes what is described as "a break in the life cycle".

As recently as April 1969 the newspapers reported a further bizarre version of the mirror story, the case of a young couple who felt it necessary to secure the blessing of their home by a clergyman because their mirror had begun, without any physical reason, to reflect a six-inch dagger.

In some of these very common day-to-day superstitions may be seen the expressions of certain basic attitudes to life and death, which are apparently unvarying from age to age. The belief that coming events cast their shadows before, is so implicitly accepted by the vast majority of mankind that precisely the same symbolic occurrences which disturbed our more openly superstitious ancestry recur constantly in our own experience, subject of course to certain minor modifications produced by change in the environment. That a falling picture presages a death in the family is an old wives' tale with a vast number of modern believers, but it has an extremely interesting background and throws light on the reason for its survival as a superstition. It is one of the fundamental principles of magic that a replica or likeness of any object contains something of the inherent qualities of the original and is in effect like the reflection in the mirror, another soul. A portrait belongs completely to this category for from the standpoint of the magic it *is* the original. Acceptance of this doctrine lies at the root of the still not yet extinct superstition that to be photographed is unlucky since this places the soul of the person photographed within the power of the photographer. Most people are aware of this superstition that a falling picture portends a death in the house. Originally this referred only to the person portrayed but in its present form any individual in the household is a possible victim.

A strongly held modern household superstition, and one that shows no sign of banishment, relates to the peacock symbol, which is unlucky solely because in the past the eyes in its tail were reminiscent to the peasant mind of the evil eye. For this reason Oriental tables with their peacock design are not always welcome in the house. In the words of one Devonshire housewife known to the author : "Peacocks are all right outside the house but they must never be brought inside." Sometimes the fear of this beautiful bird can be carried to extraordinary lengths as when a garage owner of the author's acquaintance, whose business had gone into decline, ordered the destruction of an inlaid table with a peacock motif, one of his wife's most cherished possessions. A publisher who had considered promoting a paperback venture with a peacock motif was wise enough to listen to the warnings of a superstition-conscious public relations officer and to adopt another, less intimidating, design.

China ornaments of the animal variety must always face in the general direction of the room and never the door or "the luck will run out of the house". This ritual is directly associated with that old-time staple of our economy, wool, for the superstition applied originally to china sheep in the main and only later became transferred to other objects. The reasoning behind this superstition can perhaps be best explained by the formula : wool is wealth, therefore if a sheep should look in your direction wealth will be coming your way; contrariwise, if it looks elsewhere the luck cannot reach you. By turning the china sheep towards himself, the house-owner hoped to attract good luck and wealth into his own hands.

It would not normally be expected that the lighting of a modern house could have any place whatsoever in the category of superstitious do's and don'ts, but this is in fact the case, for there are many people who regard with distinct aversion the placing of three lamps together in a room, and this is even more odd when one considers that three is traditionally a lucky number. There is however a distinct relationship between this superstitious fear and the better known one of lighting three cigarettes with the same match; in fact the latter is responsible for the former. So far as is known the three-match superstition had its inception in the Slavonic tradition that only a priest could light the three candles at the altar without invoking the anger of the god, while for a layman to do so was disastrous. From this it was but a step to the Russian peasant superstition that lighting a pipe with three matches brought misfortune, a phobia that was later adopted by British soldiers fighting in the Crimea, who regarded the lighting of three cigarettes from the same match as an invitation to death from a sniper's bullet, and which entered popular currency at about the time of the Boer War. Once three lights had been accepted as an invocation of death it was only a matter of time before the superstition became extended to other types of illumination, firstly candles, and now electric lights.

In the modern world some superstitions, like everything else, tend to be adopted on impulse, become temporarily the rage and then be discarded without ceremony. Into this class falls the bed-orientation fetishes which are oddly enough assumed to have some scientific basis for their existence. Some sleepers insist that their heads and feet must lie in a north/south direction in line with the magnetic pole, or that the bed must always be placed in alignment with the floorboards and never across them. And there are those who assiduously place blocks of wood beneath the bottom of the bed, acting on the principle that the head must always occupy a lower position than the feet. Now whether the orientation of an individual at rest has any tangible influence upon his health is a point that has never been made the subject of conclusive investigation; nevertheless it is assumed by those who follow the practices described above that they are founded upon scientific principles. This may well be the case, however, for certain primitive communities, particularly in North and South America, always observed strict rules of orientation in the construction of their villages. In our own day the scientifically-conscious Danish pig industry has constructed experimental farms where every hut is designed to face in an east/west direction in an attempt to discover whether a specific alignment can have any influence upon the health of the animal.

Scientific speculations aside, it is generally taken for granted that one's state of mind when rising from bed is of supreme importance in determining one's attitude to the day ahead. In the past, when each day was considered to be an entity on its own, pregnant with remarkable possibilities, the most elaborate attempts were undertaken to penetrate the mystery of the yet unborn hours. These largely consisted of reading from one's state of mind, at the time of rising, certain signs and portents from which it might be possible to construct in advance the prospects of the day ahead. To this we are indebted for the prevailing superstition that if you believe it to be a day either earlier or later in the week than it really is, your relations with others will be affected. Thus the jingle,

> Lose a day, you lose a friend
> Gain a day, you gain a friend.

Starting the day right is the underlying principle behind the well-known superstition that if immediately upon rising every article of clothing comes instantly to hand without dropping, the day is destined to be lucky for you.

Superstition is an elusive sprite, deceptive yet somehow always operating under cover of some apparently innocent guise. Who would have believed before the introduction of the telephone that this would become a focal point for extra-sensory perception, for many people now claim to be aware in advance that their telephone will ring. Extremely ill-omened is the sound of a telephone bell ringing intermittently with no incoming call following it but this can surely be traced to the old superstition that the booming sound emitted by a church bell when it had been rung by no human hand was an omen of death. Even more eccentric is the contemporary belief that it is possible to compel a friend to telephone by an act of will.

There are apparently no absolutely new superstitions but only ancient ones which, as if possessed by some diabolical instinct for survival, persist in advancing from generation to generation disguised as novelties.

It is of course within the house itself that most of our older superstitions have become firmly established in their original and undisguised form and where they have become integrated in the traditional rites of the housewife. There are many women today who regard it as extremely unlucky to turn their mattresses on a Sunday or to carry out housework of any kind on a Friday. An old lady known to the author regards Friday housework as so disaster-provoking that she finds it necessary to chant as she sweeps the charming homemade litany, "Friday, Friday, keep your nose tidy", which is in her eyes a protective charm of great psychic efficacy.

Most housewives when cleaning a room find themselves unconsciously sweeping inwards rather than towards the door and will perhaps wonder why they adopted this habit in the first place. This custom has developed as the direct outgrowth of an old and apparently universal superstition which for some unknown reason equates dust with luck or money, and has found expression in the strongly held conviction that by sweeping outwards one "sweeps the luck of the house away", this still being regarded as a sacred truth among the poorer classes, particularly by charladies. It is a superstition that has become completely extinct in households where a vacuum cleaner is used.

Another quaint old superstition still strictly observed in some rural areas of Britain today, and in particular Devon and Cornwall, holds that one must never buy a broom or brush during the month of May. The origins of this curious prohibition are closely associated with the broom, a magical plant of phallic significance, which could not be gathered during May, the Roman month of death, without some calamity falling upon the head of the transgressor. Our first domestic brooms, the besoms, were manufactured from the broom plant and it is therefore quite understandable why the next stage in evolution of this superstition should have found expression in the fear that to manufacture a broom in the fatal month brought misfortune. In modern times this superstition has overlapped its original boundaries and has spread in a number of unexpected directions. Thus in some places it is considered unlucky to purchase not only brooms but brushes also in May, and buying a toothbrush can also fall within the tabooed act. In its most recent manifestation the superstition has been extended to a strict avoidance of whitewashing ceilings in the month of May, a superstition that is common in some parts of rural Devon today. This curious taboo lies at the root of the well-known rhyme :

> If you buy a broom or a brush in May
> You'll sweeep the head of the household away.

In Cornwall there are quite a number of housewives who will never attempt to clean fruit stains from fabric until the fruit itself is in season and who believe in fact that it would be quite impossible to do so at any other time. These ladies would no doubt be astounded to discover that they are honouring one of the most venerable precepts of magic, the doctrine that there is an interconnection between an object and its parts (in this case the tree and its fruit) however distantly separated they might be.

Some north of England housewives subscribe to a custom that belongs properly to sun worship when they prepare their jams and puddings, for they make it an invariable rule always to stir the ingredients clockwise, and many really believe that to stir from right to left will threaten the success of the operation. The ancient sunworshippers always proceeded around the altar from east to west. A similar ritual is apparent in the custom of passing the port from left to right around the dinner table, and also in the clockwise circular movement of our folk dances. The name for this rotary action is "deiseal"; its opposite "widdershins" is supposed to invoke those enemies of the sun, the powers of darkness, to nullify the success of whatever operation is in hand.

One of the more surprising aspects of today's superstitious beliefs is the continued influence of the more ancient streams of magical thinking. Crossed knives on a table will rarely remain in this ominous position for long for someone will be certain to separate them within a matter of minutes. The ostensible reason for this superstition is that crossed knives portend a quarrel and this is supported by two historic facts: that in the past the dagger served as both fighting weapon and "eating iron" and that the crossing of weapons occurred in the duel. But there is a third factor to be considered, the role of iron as a magical metal with the power to transform the innocent crossing of knives into a real conflict. Then there is that other well-known custom of presenting a coin in return for the gift of a knife which is supposed to prevent the severance of the friendship, a rite that is universal today in view of the popularity of cutlery as a presentation piece. The motive behind this superstition can easily be detected once the knife is recognised as "psychologically" a potentially aggressive weapon. In this case the gift of an aggressive cutting implement endowed with a magical power threatens to sever the invisible links between the giver and recipient and thus imperils their friendship. Purchasing the knife, however, converts the transaction into a peaceful act of commerce and neutralises the psychic dangers to the friendship that would otherwise be incurred.

Fork and spoon superstitions have become almost extinct even in the really superstitious family. There exists, however, an interesting relic of hospitality lore in the belief that if a guest who is making a single visit to one's home folds his own napkin he has ritually foreordained the "folding up" of the friendship.

To spill salt is as powerful an omen of misfortune in the third quarter of the twentieth century as it was in Ancient Greece, but disaster can be offset by casting a pinch over the left shoulder "right into the Devil's face". Salt was the symbol of life in primitive communities because of its powers as a preservative, and therefore perhaps naturally became equated with all that was good. By a similar process of reasoning, decay, the "enemy" of salt, was perhaps understandably associated with the spirit of death and therefore of the Devil. Thus the minor misadventure of spilling salt was regarded as the symbolic destruction of life.

However, this dangerous possibility could be countered by casting a pinch of the life-preserving salt into the face of the evil spirit who, so our ancestors supposed, stood at our left or sinister side. There are a vast variety of salt superstitions in currency, all over the world supplying clear testimony of the undying influence of this symbol in our lives. In Yorkshire no one will pass salt directly to another, and the cellar is invariably laid on the table for the other guest to pick up. Salt is also taken into a new house in some parts of the north of England as a magic charm to bring good fortune to the household.

The fact that bread superstitions are today almost extinct is of considerable interest in that they provide an indication of the part played by environmental factors in the formation of beliefs. In the past, particularly among communities at subsistence level, any waste of food was regarded as sacrilege. Among Roman Catholics, for example, such waste was said to "make Our Lady cry" and gave rise to the Irish proverb, "If you throw away bread you will follow the crow for it." In England it was believed that to burn bread was unlucky but doubtless the last vestige of this old, superstitious fear of abusing the bounty of nature took the form of a practice observed until fairly recently in the more poverty stricken parts of the North in which every last scrap of stale bread had to be consumed entirely before the newly baked loaf could be cut. In a curious and rather pleasing little rite associated with twentieth-century tea table a girl who takes the last piece of bread and butter is often told that she will now acquire "a handsome husband or ten thousand a year". Until the last war the sum was a tenth of this amount, but it has apparently increased with the rise in the cost of living. Incredible as it might now appear, this superstition is a direct heritage of the old-time ritualism of the harvest field when the last sheaf of wheat or corn was often plaited into a "dolly" or "kern baby" and presented to one of the unmarried girls, who was then expected to acquire both a husband and money before the year was out. Thus the old magic of the peasant cornfield continues to survive disguised as a fanciful modern afternoon tea-rite.

Stirring the tea in the pot widdershins, that is from right to left, it goes without saying can cause a quarrel, while the obvious sexual symbolism of the spout is doubtless responsible for the well-known superstition that if two women pour from the same pot one of them will have a baby within a year.

From the house itself it is only a step in terms of superstition to the garden, which is still the repository of much mystical lore. This is perhaps understandable, for the art of growing things has always been associated with a kind of reverence almost pagan in its fervour. It is generally accepted that some individuals possess "green fingers" which, when one considers the matter, suggests a supernatural power over Nature, a form of command, if not kinship, between the cultivator and the things that are grown. This becomes less of a mystery when we discover that plants, flowers and trees were assumed in the not-so-distant past to be the abodes of elemental spirits or of fairies both good and bad, as for example the foxglove or "witches thimble", the symbol of insincerity. This type of belief was strongest in medieval times, but it still lives on as part of the folklore of the garden, having managed to withstand the winds of change, and it is the philosophy behind quite a number of today's flower superstitions.

In ancient Egypt a gift of flowers was regarded as a donation of good luck, a pleasant superstition that survives, in Belgium for example, at the present time and it is understandable therefore why flowers should still have symbolic value for many people.

Marigolds, being flowers of the sun, are luck-bringers and can be brought into the home. On the other hand the daffodil, beloved of Wordsworth, was once used as a substitute for human sacrifice, and for this forgotten reason is still sometimes kept from the house in the north-east of England, as occasionally are its bulbs in the south of the country. The rose, symbol of love, also brings luck, and a bouquet of these flowers should always be carried by a bride on her wedding day. Purple flowers are reputed to bring financial luck to the home. The white carnation is a well-known symbol of admiration and in the language of flowers means "I offer chaste love". Heavily scented flowers are suggestive of funerals, hence their unlucky reputation, while red and white flowers are studiously kept from the home for another forgotten reason, for in Roman times red and white roses were laid on the graves of lovers. Mimosa in the home is a death-bringer, and white lilac is often rejected by florists as a hospital flower because of its close association with funerals.

The bulk of the more melancholy type of flower superstitions arise from the curious peasant belief that some flowers were the homes of the souls of the dead, a superstition both beautiful and

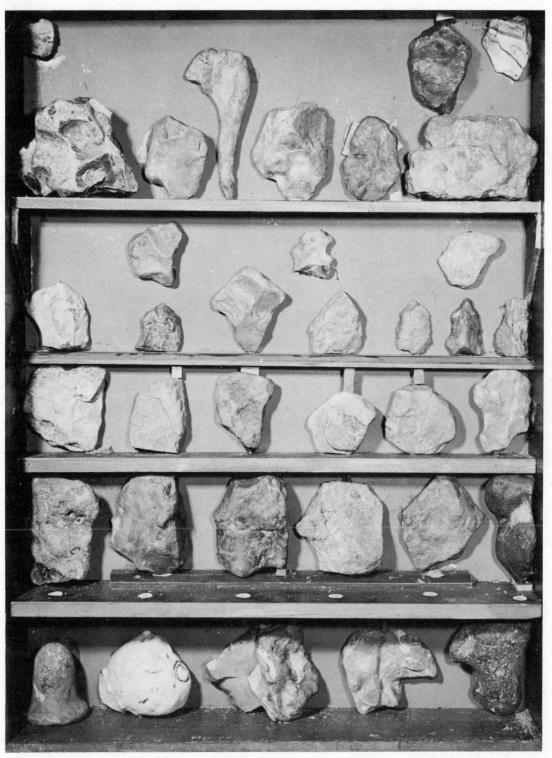

Curious collection of "magic stones"—a countryman's lucky charms.

Proverbially shoes, new or old, spell death if placed on a table.

pagan in its simplicity. The real reason why it is considered unlucky to bring May (hawthorn) into the house is because in pagan times men and women intended for sacrifice were crowned with May blossom. It is also thought unlucky to bring the first snowdrop of the year into the house, owing to its shroud-like appearance.

For vegetable growers there is a certain amount of lore which perhaps ought to be taken into account when cultivating the garden plot. Parsley was associated in classical times with the spirit of death but our resourceful ancestors thoughtfully side-stepped this dangerous aspect by confining the sowing of the seed to a holy day, Good Friday. The lettuce, which is still thought of as a remedy for sterility, was in Roman times used as an aphrodisiac. The tomato, which was once reputed to have a similar power, was for this reason known as the love apple and was in consequence in great demand. However those dedicated enemies of passion, the Puritans, decided to give the tomato a bad name by declaring it to be a deadly poison and only in fairly recent times has it been rehabilitated. Incidentally it is customary to make a wish when eating new potatoes in deference to the old belief that the time of the first emergence of any living thing is highly propitious for the granting of earthly desires.

Our gardens of today are no longer placed under the protection of some classical goddess, an Aphrodite or an Undine, but in their place householders have adopted plastic gnomes both as garden ornaments and as luck-bringers. This is of course as it should be, for these small Germanic goblins, although in fact somewhat out of their native element, for they were originally subterranean elementals, are the traditional guardians of treasures.

Every now and again a little of that older stratum of garden lore comes to the surface, as in the example confided to the author by a green-fingered housewife of Market Bosworth to the effect that "mushrooms thrive on a woman's love" and that "a flower blooming out of season is an omen of death". It is also apparent that some of these older superstitions are about to receive the benediction of science, for an American research foundation has discovered that roses are apparently subject to emotions of jealousy, and that burning leaves exhibit distinct symptoms of distress. Under these circumstances it is perhaps not over-surprising that a theory has now been advanced by a Russian scientist to the effect that plants have the power of communicating with one another. Doubtless in the course of time it will be possible to discover by direct questioning of our garden flowers what particular tragic or joyful event in their romantic history was responsible for their acquiring the reputation of being either lucky or unlucky charmers.

Despite the fact that our theologians have always insisted that animals are without souls, cats and dogs seem to have acquired a reputation for supernatural qualities of a high order. Few would have the audacity to question whether dogs are good judges of character, and most will testify to the ability of these animals to sense death before it actually takes place and to their power to see ghosts, concerning which so many anecdotes are told. In the words of one dedicated animal worshipper: "Animals are psychic beings and to understand them properly you must be psychic yourself."

How then, one may well wonder, did this remarkable attitude to the animal kingdom ever develop in the first place? The answer lies almost certainly in the primitive approach to all forms of non-human life, which treats animals as denizens of a psychic domain, completely outside and alien to the world of man, and representative of the elemental powers of nature. For this reason animals were often selected as clan totems and gods, and even after domestication much of this supernatural reputation has survived in the superstitious approach to the dog, which if dog-owners are to be believed often returns to its old home as a ghost. The domestic cat, which was the emblem of Bast, Cat-Goddess of the ancient Egyptian city of Bubastes, was worshipped as a deity by the ancient Egyptians and this is almost certainly responsible for the aura of magic with which it has been surrounded ever since. It was no doubt this pagan aspect which resulted in the degradation of this luckless animal into the witch's familiar in the sixteenth and seventeenth centuries. Today we have a number of superstitious beliefs associated with the black cat (black being the supposed colour of the powers of darkness), which is generally regarded as a kind of highly charged magical battery with the ability to influence the affairs of man for good or ill. This is why it is lucky for a black cat to walk towards you, for in so doing it conveys prosperity in your direction, while the reverse applies should it walk the other way. In the United States and parts of Europe, however, the black cat is ostracised as a symbol of disaster, doubtless because of its supposed past association with black witchcraft. There are a number of surviving superstitions associated with the black cat which suggest a similar dual role in our own history.

Many mothers still refuse to permit a cat anywhere near a sleeping baby in case it should be smothered by the animal sitting on its face, but this fear is in part influenced by the old belief that cats killed babies by "sucking their breath" and this in turn was derived from an even older belief that the cat was a kind of vampire. In its latest manifestation the same old superstition has re-emerged in medical garb and many people insist that the breath of a cat can cause cancer. On the other hand the cat is a strong luck-bringer in Cornwall, where it is still believed that wishes can be made to come true by the simple process of stroking the back of a black cat three times, using three fingers only.

Doubtless in times past when each well-to-do household sported its pony trap there existed a host of superstitions associated with the horse. Today, however, with the replacement of this animal by horse-power we have in the householder's mobile shrine the automobile a focal point for a vast new area of magical concepts, some the heritage of horse and buggy days but others largely revised versions of even older magical concepts.

It is of course only to be expected that a superstitious individual will apply his own peculiar mystical attitude to whatever operation he happens to be engaged in at the time, and this is particularly apparent in the case of motoring with its ever-present possibilities of accident and even death, and this creates a perfect breeding ground for superstitious fears.

It is perhaps for this reason that motorists are careful to avoid the use of a sinister word like "accident", apparently from the half belief that its mere utterance must in some mysterious way enhance the likelihood of danger. Similarly there is always great reluctance to boast of an accident-free record, for this represents an open invitation to the devils of disaster to strike the motorist down—yet another variation on the theme of "tempting providence". There are, in addition, a number of other minor fetishes peculiar to motoring, as for example the belief that good fortune on the road can be maintained by the transference of some object from an old and lucky car to a new one at the time of purchase. These might consist of an old pair of driving gloves, or on occasion a lucky Irish penny which is normally kept in the ashtray.

Sometimes it is the picture of a loved one, and occasionally a genuine lucky charm. A brief investigation carried out by the author into the mythology of the private motorist brought to light a surprising variety of superstitions which, despite their modern veneer, bear every sign of great antiquity.

Motorists, especially women, still have a considerable aversion to picking up a new car on Friday the thirteenth, since by doing so they imagine themselves condemned to endless mechanical trouble and even accidents. A happy experience with a first car will frequently prompt an owner to purchase the same make time and time again, on the principle of "change the car : change the luck".

That accidents always run in threes is firmly believed by motorists and pedestrians alike.

The second-hand cars of the rich are often in demand by those who believe that some of the luck of the original owner will rub off on to themselves.

For obvious reasons it is still commonly held unlucky to count the cars following a hearse to a funeral.

Oddly enough, the broken looking-glass superstition does not seem to apply in the case of the damaged wing-mirror, as far as the great majority of motorists are concerned.

A modern superstition, and one that is accepted by almost every motorist, is what can only be described as the car-washing fetish. A vast number of motorists religiously insist that a cruel Providence stands by until they have completed washing their cars before sending down a shower of rain upon their automobiles. Little do they realise that they have become the victims of a superstition which emanated from modern America, the home of the automobile. It is one of the basic rules of magic that by imitating an event you can actually make it happen. A well-known example is the tribal rainmaker who, in times of drought, pours water upon the parched earth as a hint to the rain gods to follow suit. The motorist, when washing his car, is doing precisely the same thing and therefore half expects the same end product, and of course is rarely disappointed. He also invites the hostility of the gods by presuming upon fate.

There also exists today a very emphatic belief in "jinx" cars, these being perfectly roadworthy vehicles that are for some inexplicable reason accident-prone, this being perhaps one of the most remarkable expressions of diabolical possession that this age can offer. Once a car has acquired a bad name its owner almost expects it to live up—or rather down—to its reputation, and sooner or later an almost neurotic relationship will develop between the two. However, in the words of one dealer, perhaps "there are no jinx cars; only jinx drivers".

In the selection of car numbers most motorists have a preference for those traditional luck-bringers three, seven and nine, and combinations of these, which being odd numbers are under the protection of the gods. They studiously avoid using combinations amounting to thirteen, however. In the main motorists rest perfectly secure against all dangers, real or imagined, in the arms of that popular saint-cum-lucky-charm, St. Christopher, who despite his recent demotion and subsequent reappointment by the Papal authorities continues to carry out his traditional role as the protector of travellers on the road.

CHAPTER III

WORK AND TRAVEL

MAN at his work is as much a prey to superstitious fears as the housewife in her home, although rapid changes in the conditions of modern industrial and commercial life have tended to make the older type of tradition with its associated superstitions less common as the economic revolution proceeds. It would be almost impossible today, for example, to discover very much of the folklore of the older trades, for craftsmanship has long been in the melting pot and where it has not become completely dissolved it has been transformed almost beyond recognition. Lost today are those once clearly defined types of tradition distinguishing crafts that were once practised in common like carpentry and masonry, and the individual rites of craftsmen like the tailor who so often worked alone. Industry itself, after displacing the traditional craftsmen, has witnessed a continuous succession of technical revolutions in which the industrialised craftsman has been displaced by the mechanic, who in turn has been forced to give way to the technician, who in *his* turn is in process of being displaced at an ever accelerating tempo by the electronics revolution. Gone, alas, forever are those old crafts with their highly individual lore and peculiar superstitions—the millers, the bakers, the spinners, the weavers and those masters of fire the blacksmiths, who were often regarded almost as magicians along with the woodcutters and charcoal burners. Even the village healer, once the centre of vast arcana of magic and mystery, has long retreated before the advance of scientific medicine, although his successor the "fringe-medicine man" is very much in vogue among city dwellers.

Work-superstitions follow an unvarying pattern, though, despite all these revolutionary changes. If superstition continues to be strongly entrenched in any particular occupation it is because of the existence of a deeply rooted sense of insecurity, whether real or imagined, creating a social climate in which omens and portents may be read into quite ordinary occurrences, and one in which, to a considerable extent, the past is allowed to dominate the present.

In times of bad trade, to take an example, the well-known superstition that a pair of shoes placed on a table is a harbinger of death, which is in fact based upon the ancient custom of laying a pair of new shoes on a coffin, is suddenly adapted to meet the new situation, for it is then regarded as a sign of forthcoming unemployment. Carpenters have been known to refuse to brush shavings from their benches when trade is bad since this to their minds symbolises "brushing the work away". Small shopkeepers who are dependent entirely upon their own efforts for their economic survival often believe that by sweeping "away from the shop front" first thing in the morning they sweep away a whole day's trade. Dressmakers defer to this superstition in their own way with the maxim, "Dust the table with a piece of paper and you dust away the work". Whether dressmakers still observe the old rite of spitting on the outside of a finished work is highly doubtful, despite the acknowledged power of human spittle to dispel bad luck, but there still survives a latent belief that the left sleeve must always be attended to before the right when sewing a border on to a garment. A further example is the aversion felt by workers in the "rag trade" to twisting a coat-hanger round and round by its wire holder, as this suggests the winding-up of the business.

Included in the category of old-style and easily recognisable superstitions is the very general belief that it is dangerous to whistle at one's job, "since this whistles away the work", in the same way that the seaman regards whistling aboard ship as encouraging rough seas by summoning an unwanted storm. It would therefore appear that the more chancy the operation, be it a private or social one, the more necessary it is to the peace of mind of the individual that he should avoid certain acts, the performance of which, so he has been taught, will bring down upon his head the thing that he most fears. He is unconsciously making the case for magic by testifying to a private belief that by a ritual movement, as with a broomstick or by the avoidance of certain practices, it is possible to exercise a measure of control over fate.

Industrial life, in so far as it represents security of employment, provides an environment less congenial to the old type of "fear" superstition than in the past. But even in the vast factory complex there are islands of mystery as frightening to certain individuals as any tabooed shrine of a pagan faith. One accepts, of course, that some individuals will be more accident-prone than others and for this there is indeed actuarial support. But how is one to regard the sincere belief among many industrial workers that an individual has become a jinx solely because he has a record of accident-proneness in consequence of which men will be reluctant to work with him? There are "jinx" machines, too, from power looms to machine tools, which, like the traditional dog with a bad name, constantly live up to their ill-omened reputations for creating trouble or accidents, and which workmen will strenuously avoid using. Here in a completely modern setting is expressed one of our most primitive superstitions, the belief that an inanimate object can acquire not only a form of life of its own but almost human characteristics. Out of this type of thinking grew the ancestral worship of trees, of spirits in rivers and lakes, and of the concept of the trolls of Scandinavia who were no more than personifications of the rocks. Once we accept that a machine possesses any type of intelligence independent of its operator we are well on the road back to magic.

The role of tradition and custom in social thinking has been the subject of a great deal of study, but the influence of superstition on industrial affairs has received very little attention for the simple reason that it has hitherto been nobody's business to investigate superstitions other than as nonsensical relics of folk belief. The day might well arrive when no time-and-motion study would be complete without its comprehensive survey of the superstition inspired aspects of a worker's behaviour. A perfect example would be the window cleaner whose work involves all the elements necessary to a superstitious state of mind : he is an individual worker, self-employed, subject to vagaries of weather, and constantly at risk from falling from heights. Most window cleaners follow a system of beliefs which, as can be seen, consist of an extremely interesting combination of sense, self-awareness and supernaturalism.

1. "If before starting the day's work you *feel* something wrong is likely to happen don't risk climbing the ladder. Take a day off."
2. "Never begin work on the same spot where another window cleaner has fallen from a ladder."
3. "Once you've established a method for erecting a cradle for window cleaning never change it. To do so brings bad luck.

These apparently superstitious attitudes come almost second nature to men whose daily routine involves the risk of life and limb. Who is to say therefore that since they have become psychologically necessary they can properly be divorced from the function of window cleaning?

As might be expected, the steeplejack, whose work involves similar risks, reacts in like manner to the possibilities of accident; it is not uncommon for him to twist his braces as a kind of psychic insurance against a fall, for twisting is no more than a variant of knot-tying which, in magic the world over, has always symbolised security. In marriage we find the knot represented in the term "the bonds of matrimony" and in most situations of possible danger it secures the mind against the fear of disaster. Without the benefit of this elementary precaution there are many workmen who would not care to expose their lives to danger.

Some months ago a newspaper in reporting some of the idiosyncracies of working life described another tradition in the story of two light-hearted steeplejacks who had celebrated the erection of a 250-feet chimney by suspending a pair of crimson panties from its summit, much to the annoyance of the factory owner; as they explained at the time this was their traditional "topping out" ceremony. Topping out was originally one of the superstitious rites of the building trade, a method of placing a newly built house under the protection of a guardian tree was set up on the roof. It has long been extinct as a popular custom, however, although in recent years there has been an attempt by some of the larger building firms to revive it for publicity purposes. In 1961 at Colindale an enormous garland of laurel flowers and pieces of coloured material was erected on a roof, and some time later a treetop was set up on a building at Leytonstone. The custom of itself would be of little contemporary interest but for the fact that during a topping out ceremony at the Smithfield Poultry Market in 1962 a workman explained to the Press that its purpose was to "ward off evil spirits and to protect those who were to occupy the buildings from bad luck".

The building trade, in the pagan past, was responsible for some extremely bloody rites in deference to the superstition that a fee in blood had to be paid to the earth deity by those who occupied any part of her territory. Young children were often buried in the foundations of bridges and other buildings, as at the Roman fort at Reculver, but later the custom became humanised and animals and then coins were laid beneath the foundation stone instead, this being traditionally sited at the N.E. *corner.* The civic official who places a luck-bringing token coin beneath the corner stone of a modern building is blissfully unaware of the gruesome origins of this popular custom, or of the distantly-related superstition that it is unlucky to live in a corner house.

Never fill your jam-jar before you've caught your first fish.

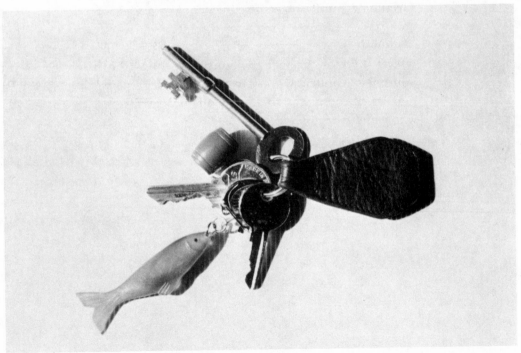

The fish as the symbol of life and abundance is a luck-bringer.

Knocking on wood began with touching a tree trunk, to draw on its supernatural powers.

Bridge builders are apparently far more superstitious today than other members of the building industry. One of the more celebrated of these, who must of necessity be nameless, was recently reported as saying that it was unwise to talk or write about a bridge-building project, as disaster always followed. To use his own words quoted from a newspaper article : "Sure enough the thing falls down. I don't think the King's Bridge at Melbourne would have collapsed if the engineer hadn't written a series of articles about the design. The ink was hardly dry before the bridge fell in the drink. Take the Frejus Dam disaster. A Frenchman had written a paper to be read in London. His speech ended with him saying something like : 'We learn from our mistakes'. Two days before the paper was due to be given the dam collapsed."

What our twentieth-century bridge builder is actually saying is that it is tempting Providence to announce publicly the completion of a building enterprise. In doing so, however, he merely echoes one of the more deep-seated superstitions of the human race, i.e. that to announce the completion of any operation or constructional project is tantamount to inviting the gods to knock it down again. For this reason it was long a custom among superstitious builders never to cement the last brick of a house into place. The gods have always looked with a jaundiced eye upon all constructional enterprises from the Tower of Babel onwards. Architects, incidentally, have their own superstitions. Some take the view that to say thoughtlessly, "Well, that's the *end* of the job" is likely to put them out of work.

The life of the miner, despite modern mechanisation, continues to be dangerous today in the way that life at sea has largely ceased to be. For this reason many mining superstitions have survived relatively intact, whereas most marine ones are in process of dissolution. In common with the seaman, however, the miner studiously avoids whistling when down the mine. The original and forgotten reason for this was that it annoyed the "knockers" or subterranean spirits. Miners also refuse to tolerate a cat in the mine, and the use of the word itself is tabooed, for this animal is generally regarded as a harbinger of disaster. If, after leaving his home for work, the miner finds he has to interrupt his journey and return for any reason, he will knock three times on the window for whatever he wants, since to re-enter the house is unlucky. Another old mining superstition, albeit in disguised form, is a fear of the evil eye. Despite the improvements in medical care the occasional cross-eyed individual is still sometimes seen, but to the miner this is the worst of omens.

Therefore he either crosses to the other side of the road to "cross out" the misfortune, or he may even abandon work for that day.

Even a random examination of the superstitions of men at work can bring to light some extraordinary practices which a psychiatrist might classify as phobias. A streetmarket stallholder religiously spits on the first coin received in any day in the hope that it will then be augmented by many others. Spittle is the traditional elixir for enhancing the good influences and for neutralising hostile ones; handsel money, as the first coin received in the market is called, is spat upon as a magical rite to ensure commercial success.

A market worker acquaintance of the author's actually took in his stride the superstitious phobias of his customers, mainly West Indians—and in particular their reluctance to purchase green socks—by organising a working arrangement with another market man in a predominantly Irish district for the exchange of all unsold stock of green socks for the latter's surplus red ones, this being a colour always popular with Negroes. Despite the decline in this oldest of superstitions, the fear of green can often exert an important influence commercially, particularly among the poorer classes where tradition maintains its strongest hold. A hotwater bottle manufacturer in the mid-sixties discovered, for example, that sales resistance to the green variety was still a factor to be reckoned with, while a sweet manufacturer discovered to his amazement that his green jelly babies were less in favour than those of other colours in the north of England—always a hotbed of the older superstitions. At the root of this fear lies the ancient terror of adopting the colour of the green-clad elementals as this was supposed to place one in their power.

The terror of boasting or of anticipating the completion of an event is an influence permeating every type of work involving tension or anxiety. A shop girl or salesman hesitates before dating the first sales voucher in advance in case there will be no sales. Authors are reluctant to discuss the book upon which they are engaged from a hidden fear that by so doing they may hinder its completion. Clerks will refuse to turn over the daily calendar before the day itself has arrived.

Magic will sometimes manifest itself in the most remarkable ways. The author himself became aware of the insidious influence of superstition in his life when he was presented with a toy black cat by a well-wisher. He found that by degrees the cat began to assume the qualities of a mascot, so much so that when one of its legs was damaged he felt a momentary sensation of alarm. All creative workers run the risk of being influenced by omens and so apparently are waiters and diners. The black cat motif is strongly emphasised in the ritual observed by the Savoy Hotel in London which never seats its diners down thirteen to a table. If a thirteenth place has been ordered the waiter lays a wooden effigy of a cat called Kaspar at the thirteenth spot.

A photographer recently disclosed to the author the superstitious phobias of some of his customers and in doing so revealed his own. Portraiture throughout history has provided a focal point for magical beliefs of all kinds, being concerned with images which, as explained earlier in discussing the falling-picture superstition, are in effect second souls or doubles. There are still backward communities in Africa and elsewhere where individuals refuse to be photographed on principle since this, to their minds, involves the capture of their individual souls by the photographer. Among current urban photographic superstitions is the refusal by some brides to be photographed prior to the wedding since this seems to be tempting fate by anticipation. At the same time there is apparently a growing tendency among the old to have their photographs taken shortly before their deaths. This, my photographer insisted, indicated an instinctive awareness on the part of the sitters of what fate held in store for them. More likely, however, it is no more than an updated and upturned version of a superstition common in the early days of the camera and which still lingers on, to the effect that those who are photographed may expect to die shortly, which in itself is yet another version of the age-old fear felt by primitive man at the possible capture of his reflection or soul.

Car salesmen, who are often acutely aware of the superstitious attitudes of some of their customers are subject to superstitions of their own of which they are usually unconscious. Many have a decided aversion to touching a car in which they are aware someone has died. Others are prepared to admit that a car, like a house, can have a distinctive "atmosphere" of its own. Some will even subscribe to the theory that there are lucky and unlucky cars.

Even the most solid citizens are liable to become the secret slaves of one or other mystical belief. Motor-cyclist policemen have a strong objection to anyone touching their crash helmets, for this is the barrier that stands between the rider and death. Unlike the layman the police officer does not have the freedom to deck his uniform with the protective charms and amulets that are worn by the ton-up boys of the road. As one might expect some policemen, because of the hazardous nature of their work, tend to be extremely superstitious, and in one amusing case a very efficient police constable went the whole hog and became a dedicated member of a witch coven. Another became a psychic healer in his off-duty hours, while yet another retired from the Force to take up ghost-story writing and investigation as a full-time profession.

To follow the superstitious thread through every trade and profession would be pointless for it must be obvious that a very similar pattern prevails in all of them. There are, or perhaps were, exotic eccentricities that make the superstition-hunters' job infinitely rewarding; such as when an old gas-worker was found to have suspended around his neck an amulet in the shape of a piece of coke in a leather bag, to ward off chest complaints.

It might be of interest, however, to consider the superstitious processes as they affect the world of commerce and which influence the behaviour of a surprisingly large number of those involved in the hazardous game of money-making. The business-man will often maintain a very precise daily route on his way to his office, perhaps keeping strictly to the right-hand footpath and entering the railway station by the same gateway. Like 99% of humanity he will avoid walking under a ladder, an unlucky symbol because of the association of the ladder with the old time gallows. This is very often his personal magical routine for "starting the day right", an essential procedure if fate is to smile upon his plans. If he happens to be an accountant he will doubtless be aware of the "jinx" account, the portfolio which creates a sense of trouble even before it has even been opened, and which invariably lives down to its reputation. If he is a newspaper man he will most probably be party to the office superstition that the foreign desk will almost certainly be unoccupied on the particular day that a news bombshell bursts overseas, a superstition that is known in the United States, for some forgotten reason as "Murphy's law". Should he happen to be involved in high finance he will be even more aware of the need to avoid Friday the 13th for board meetings. It has in fact been established that very few such meetings are convened on this date, doubtless in deference to the pagan goddess Frigg to whom Friday was originally dedicated and also of course because Friday was the day that Adam and Eve were expelled from Eden, the day when Christ was crucified and also because thirteen has been an unpropitious number for any gathering ever since the thirteen met at the Last Supper. In old-time Europe incidentally criminals were always executed on a Friday.

Few commercial concerns are as likely to be as overwhelmed by superstition, however, as the Huddersfield woollen manufacturer who retained five Swiss frogs in a case for consultation in times of doubt, and whose croaks in response to the questions asked them were regarded as psychic endorsement of a particular line of policy. With this in mind no one should be over surprised by the discovery that stockbrokers who, as professional risk-takers are usually in the front row of the superstitious, should consult clairvoyants and astrologers as a normal if somewhat furtive aspect of business life. According to one financial journal a prominent occultist is so heavily in demand today as a business consultant that it has become necessary to commute between London and New York. Spiritualist mediums also draw a considerable proportion of their fees from advice given to businessmen, and in this respect should be regarded more properly as fortune-tellers. No one, least of all myself, would suggest that astrologers are necessarily superstitious individuals themselves; in actual fact they claim to represent a science but in trading upon the superstitions of others they apparently succeed in extracting a considerable amount of money from the more anxious members of the commercial world. Astrology today has to be reckoned with as an economic factor of considerable importance since the stars apparently now decide our business affairs.

The computer horoscope industry has more recently become a multi-million dollar enterprise in the United States and according to a Press report one such concern anticipates an annual sale of half a million horoscopes in respect of "children, personnel directors and business corporations". Astral advice on mergers and takeovers is a speciality in this field. In the words of one brochure : "Company astrology is destined to branch out into the open".

The superstitious businessman may react in a number of ways to guidance received from the other world. Typical perhaps is the reaction of one client who declared : "I must settle my business deals this week as after that I know my stars will be against me."

The strength of the occultist business adviser lies, of course, in the reluctance of his client to disclose his gullibility to the world should the prognostications let him down, for no man will readily admit to the kind of wrong-headedness that invites ridicule. It is somewhat odd that the course of a planned economy should in this age of the computer be left in the hands of the psychic tipster, one who in times past would have been classed as a practitioner of white magic or at worst a witch.

Even the most hard-headed economic determinist might be prompted to pause at what the fates have to offer in the pages of a popular occult magazine. Between general advice ranging from clairvoyance, trance mediumship and infallible lucky charms, one discovers psychic guidance on business problems, travel and finance, but perhaps most stimulating of all is the offer of "commercial guidance" in exchange for a small fee, despatched in a stamped addressed envelope accompanied by several hairs from the client's head.

To move from the superstitions of the land to the sea is today a venture into the known rather than the unknown contrary to what is generally assumed to be the case.

Most topical works on superstitions encourage the belief that life and work at sea continue to be dominated by the most sensational of our surviving beliefs. Two generations ago this might well have been the case, but today maritime superstitions tend to be dormant among seamen and manifest themselves only in special circumstances. And why is this so? The answer is completely in keeping with what we know about the mind. The sea, having ceased to be an area of acute danger, no longer provides a field of psychological disturbance and therefore becomes free of superstitious terrors.

In the days of sail, when a voyage was for the most part a venture into the unknown, one could appreciate the sentiment that forbade that long last look at the ship as it disappeared over the horizon; since this, in terms of superstition, meant that the seaman and his sweetheart would never be reunited in this world. Furthermore, until the advent of wireless telegraphy, the seaman was often almost as completely cut off from communication with the land as if he were dead. The environmental conditions were then ideal for the creation and maintenance of a vast system of psychic protective devices, some highly individual in character and others of the collective type. Rituals had then to be observed to the letter and taboos were ignored only at one's peril. Every feature of sky and sea played its part in the curious philosophy that dominated the seafarer's life. Seagulls, which represented the souls of drowned sailors, were sacrosanct at sea, while the inshore gull that brushed its wings against the window of the sailor's cottage indicated to his household that he was in danger of drowning. This superstition corresponds to the still prevalent landsman's belief that a forthcoming death in a family will be indicated by a bird pecking at the window pane. For a mop or a bucket to fall overboard at sea was always ominous, since these symbolised the death of both sailor and ship. Loaning an object from one ship to another is still discouraged since it represents the transfer of part of a ship's good fortune. Rats were supposed to abandon the doomed ship, and gales, as already stated, could be summoned by anyone who thoughtlessly whistled.

Today, as far as the British Isles are concerned, it is largely among fishermen that the older beliefs survive with any strength, doubtless because their working life still involves a considerable degree of hazard combined with the added factor that a successful haul must always be a matter of chance. If the belief that boys are born at high tide and girls at low is at a low ebb, there is, on the other hand, still some support for the superstition that a sick person who, passing through a crisis, lives beyond the change of tide will not die until the tide has again turned. This tendency to link the fate of man with the rhythm of his environment seems to play an integral part in superstition. A very modern fishing boat builder, who avowed himself to be unsuperstitious, confided to the author during a short conversation his conviction that "Tides, especially neap tides, affect the mental outlook; moon and high tides mean lunacy, lowest ebb tide suicide".

There are fisher families, however, who subscribe to undisguised superstitions belonging to the days of old when the powers of darkness were thought to threaten every action involving a seaman's life. To point with the finger to a ship at sea marks it out for death; two black cats aboard a ship bring bad luck. Tyneside trawlermen regard the seagulls that follow their craft as signs of luck. In the West Country women and clergymen are often considered ominous passengers, the one being a possible witch, the other an enemy of the pagan sea-gods, and at Newlyn in Cornwall more than one fisher family sews copper nails into its pillows as luck-bringers. In the main, however, the fisherman, like the traveller ashore, relies for protection upon his St. Christopher medallion. In common with the cautious motorist who avoids using the word "accident" his counterpart eschews the word "drowning". At Whitby even today "pig", once a totem animal, is a tabooed word and pork is unpopular as food in some fisher families.

Among the superstitions of modern fisher folk collected by the author in the coastal villages bordering the North Sea and in the West of England there are many which indicate a strong belief in the psychic significance of minor occurrences, as for example, the curious bell-like note sometimes emitted by a tumbler or wine-glass, which is clearly associated in the fisherman's mind with the tolling of a death bell and is therefore suggestive of shipwreck. There exists also a strange terror of discovering the boat's earthenware basin upside down, or its hatch the wrong way up, since this suggests that the boat will itself turn turtle. For this reason skippers will some-times refuse to put to sea on the day that such a discovery is made. The fishing boat itself, in common with ships the world over, must be launched according to strict rites and ceremonies if its fortune is to be secured against disaster. At Appledore in Devon there is a pleasing custom in which trawlers and sailing drifters are decked with laurel leaves and woodland flowers on the occasion of the launching. It is not generally realised that the customary ship christening ceremony with its bottle of champagne displaced the earlier ritual murder of a boy who was offered as blood sacrifice to the sea gods in pre-Christian times.

The naming of any ship is of supreme importance, for its whole future can be threatened by the selection of a name that is ill-omened. Once given a name this must never be changed for this also brings disaster. A ship with a sinister reputation will even on occasion be destroyed by fire "to get rid of the death in it". The *Daily Mail* of March 20th, 1960 described how, following the Broughton Ferry disaster, the ship, which had been branded as a jinx, was ceremoniously reduced to ashes on the foreshore at night.

A liner captain will often scoff at these old-time seamen's tales but if the big ships are now free of the phobias of their smaller brethren it by no means suggests that the entire undercurrent of superstition is dead. Like the ominous raven of Nordic mythology, the superstitions have migrated to more congenial climes where death and disaster continue to overshadow the working lives of men. It is only in those danger-charged areas of the seaman's life that the old fears live on. When, in October 1969, Princess Anne and her lady-in-waiting toured a Gas Council drilling rig in the North Sea, which is always a danger point, it was reported: "No women had hitherto been allowed on to a sea rig because of the superstition that ill-luck could follow". If the superstitions of the sea are sometimes submerged, they can always be relied upon to resurface sooner or later.

The taming of the forces of nature and the reduction of the once terrifying powers of the sea, necessarily diminishes the impact of the older form of superstitions as a direct result of the elimination of the real dangers for which they are only expressions. There exists, however, a sphere of activity where all the ingredients of super-stition persist in their most dynamic form—the air. Modern air transportation, in adopting the uniform and outward ceremonial of the sea, has acquired many of its rites including the rolling-out ceremony which is based on ship christening, and the accompanying libation of champagne. At the same time a good deal of the lore of other forms of transportation has begun to insinuate into air travel. Crew and passengers alike studiously avoid using danger-charged terms like "crash" and "prang" and to the author's knowledge an air hostess who recounted a dream which had included an air crash was speedily shut up by her colleagues. There is also a strong feeling against taking flowers aboard a plane, particularly the red and white variety, which, as on land, are traditional death-bringers.

The old belief that accidents happen in threes is very strongly entrenched in aircraft mythology and it is generally accepted that a single crash must be succeeded by two further ones before the chain of disaster has run its course. An acquaintance who invariably travels by scheduled flight to South Africa was stunned upon learning that one of those planes on this particular route had crashed. He had in fact taken refuge in the illusion that the scheduled flight was accident-free and that only the charter plane was likely to be in trouble. From that time onward he studiously avoided passenger planes—until the mandatory two further crashes had occurred, and only then would he return to his normal method of travel.

As might be expected the St. Christopher medallion as well as the secret and more personal magical protective devices of the passengers are in full operation during the flight. A national newspaper recently observed : "It is fantastic to think that in the twentieth century great planes throb through the stratosphere with their passengers wearing amulets". However it is not only the passengers but the pilots who as often as not confide their future to the care of a doll or teddy bear. The more superstitious minded of passengers and crew are almost invariably those who have survived an air accident in the past. The mind of the traveller reacts very strangely to the situation of air hazard. A large number of insurance policies, for example, are taken out immediately before the plane's departure, upon the superstitious assumption, "If you insure nothing can happen but if you don't it most certainly will". It would thus appear that the air traveller often regards his insurance policy in the light of a lucky charm which suggests that the premium might be not so much a form of protection against loss through accident as a secret sacrifice to the gods. This is confirmed by a recent statement by an insurance company that most people are not only under-insured but "living on luck".

In summarising experiences in collecting the superstitions of crafts and industries one discovers that it is generally the older employee who is credited with being the most superstitious, and so it must have been all down the corridors of time. But young workers must grow old and it is perhaps then that they pause from their labours to listen to the traditional warnings of fate, and in this manner their superstitions are kept alive from generation to generation.

CHAPTER IV

RECREATION AND ENTERTAINMENT

PLAY has its own distinct set of superstitions which vary from one activity to another dependent upon the degree of tension involved. In the more competitive sports like soccer, which has long since lost its purely recreational aspect and where conflict has become the dominating aspect among player and spectator alike, ritualism has become paramount. A living mascot such as a young child is even used by some teams. On entering the field players will religiously pass the ball from the oldest to the youngest player for luck, and the ball is frequently bounced precisely three times before the team takes up its position. It is also the custom to touch the goal posts for luck. Individual players observe many private fetishes which must be religiously honoured if the day is to be won. In both soccer and rugby the left boot is usually put on before the right and the laces are generally tied in a special way. A recently published letter from a correspondent to a national newspaper disclosed how "a footballer friend of mine never starts a game without putting a new lace in his left boot, insists upon being fifth man in running on to the field and demands that his wife wave to him from the stand before the referee blows the whistle. Any slip in this ritual and he has had a bad day."

Why, one asks automatically, has such a curious complex of superstitions become part of a perfectly ordinary game? Almost certainly it is a kind of conditioned reflex arising from the memory of some past team success which has become firmly associated in the subject's mind with a series of clearly defined actions. Most of our more deeply rooted superstitions tend always to assert themselves in such a manner. Some players actually forbid their wives to watch the match on television out of fear that the game may be adversely affected, should so negative a personality as a woman cast her debilitating eye upon the proceedings.

The individual idiosyncrasies of the players are often lost sight of in the much more obvious collective hysteria of the supporting crowd. The fantastic costumes, the barbaric rattles, the hymns, songs and the rhythmic chantings, are living demonstrations of collective magic designed to banish the spectres of defeat. These have their parallels in the many individual spell-making devices which are hardly noticed amid the general excitement. A typical set of rituals carried out by a father and daughter, both football fans, came under discussion in a recent article on modern "witchcraft". In order to ensure victory it was essential that the two should follow separate routes to the football ground, should cross the road once only, enter the ground through the same turnstile and purchase their programmes from the same programme-seller. Any departure whatsoever from this strict routine spelt defeat for the home team. In the words of the interviewee, "We then know the team hasn't a hope in hell". It is not at all surprising to discover in this context that one particular nationally-known football team draws supernatural support from three followers garbed as angels, or for that matter that a football-pools punter holds his coupon up the chimney where it receives the benediction of the devil before putting it in the post.

Totemism is particularly strong in that other Anglo-Saxon religious exercise known as cricket, despite the fact that no team on earth would imperil its status with the Deity by tolerating fancy dress and rattles, let alone celestial beings in the grandstand. The collective magic of the cricket team is a secret art rarely discussed and even less frequently revealed to the uninitiated.

There is an Essex team which pins its hopes of victory on the captain's ancient cap and when this disreputable object was temporarily mislaid some time ago the team became completely dispirited and lost the next match, thereby confirming to the minds of the players the validity of their superstition. In another case, the lucky cap had to be worn by the batsmen alternately "until the score broke down". Individual cricketers tend to swear by a lucky bat. Others have been known to refuse an easy single in order to avoid a score of thirteen. The power of a fetish object whether in sport or quack medicine is invariably based upon a good testimonial. A cricketer discovers after picking up a button from the field that he has a successful innings and henceforth this object becomes his private talisman. Another, finding that success is achieved on the very day he wears a particular sweater, continues to wear it even though it has been reduced to a mass of rags and tatters. There is one well known cricketer who studiously avoids rubbing the dirty ballmarks from his bat, unconsciously testifying to the belief that to do so would rub away his luck.

Funeral rites were originally devised to offset the return of the ghost.

The serpent as the symbol of eternity protects the home against hostile spirits.

In cricket there frequently crops up the more familiar type of superstition. It is lucky to see a black cat before a match, unlucky to stumble on leaving the pavilion and even more so for the bowler to be compelled to restart his run. Extremely foreboding is the accidental strapping of the cricket pads on to the wrong legs, as this symbolises a bad start.

All ball games are ridden with superstition and this curious situation shows no signs of diminishing. Tennis fans who watch the Wimbledon crowd will be well aware of the intense visual concentration vested in the matches. It is perhaps not too surprising, therefore, to discover that optical superstitions are more strongly manifested in tennis and its fellow sport, badminton, than perhaps in any other recreation. The most common form taken by this type of superstition is the fear that by looking too intensely at one's favourite team one can threaten its success, and it is for this reason that, in times of crisis, the eyes of a superstitious onlooker will often be turned to the ground. Where there is deep emotional involvement with the outcome of a game there is a tendency to create one's own magic, as with the woman who disclosed to the writer that she felt it imperative to turn away from the television, where she had been watching a Wimbledon match, and to begin cutting the hedge, saying to herself as she did so : "If only I can finish this job in ten minutes they must win."

The tennis player, as might be expected, subscribes to a number of purely personal superstitions which are occasionally betrayed by certain rarely observed actions during the game. In 1968 it was noticeable that a Wimbledon player would never use a ball that had been returned to him after he had been faulted but always insisted upon a fresh one—in other words, a ball that had not been contaminated by bad luck.

In badminton many players seriously believe that "If you watch your side too intently they lose points", and that "If you look to the floor they pick up a load of points". And another badminton superstition : "If you find yourself successful on one particular end of the court this is a sign that it is your lucky end and you must try to start there in the next match."

It is to golf, however, that one must look for superstition and ritual in its most bizarre form. The U.S. golf professional Bert Yancey wears a copper "Voodoo Bracelet" which not only eases his aching joints but may have enabled him to win the Bing Crosby golf tournament. Of all ball games golf is the one which most resembles a religion and, to judge from the testimony of its addicts, an extremely uplifting one. In almost any clubhouse the golfer's eulogy to himself can be seen. Golf makes men good-tempered, calm and deliberate, and the dedicated player may expect to be elevated to a state of celestial bliss. The opposite is alas too often the case. Golfers are usually tense, over-eager, competitive zealots who relive each round in a kind of neurotic daydream sometimes for hours on end. It is in precisely such a milieu that one would expect to discover a vast wealth of collective and individual superstitions. Even the great Gary Player has laid down that "Superstition can be a positive force for better golf but you've got to be very sure you don't lose confidence by believing your lucky charm has let you down when your game starts to go sour".

Many golfers think it unlucky to remove the paper wrapping from a new ball once the tee has actually been reached. In teeing off the ball must be so placed that its trade name or number can be clearly seen at the top. A bad tee off is an ominous sign for the rest of the game. Number superstitions are particularly potent among golfers who tend to favour balls bearing the odd numbers three, five, seven, but less frequently nine. There are golfers who studiously avoid selecting any ball with a high number since this to their minds condemns them to a high number of strokes for each hole played.

Mascots are fairly common among golfers, a very topical example being the miniature wishing-well carried in the pocket of Tony Jacklin, winner of the 1969 Open Championship. It is quite customary for a golfer to touch or rub his mascot before playing his shot.

There are perhaps as many individual rites as there are players in golf but almost invariably they reiterate patterns of superstitious behaviour that are common elsewhere. Golfers are extremely superstitious about the colour of their clothing, but a well known golfing superstition is the refusal to mention the words "shank" or "socket", for to strike the ball with the club shank or socket is for some mysterious reason the most dreaded of all the bad habits to which golfers are prone. Whilst not actually blanching at the very thought golfers prefer to disguise its sound by using the euphemism "Lucy Locket" instead. So shocking is the forbidden word that more than one professional has been heard to protest, "Don't say it! It's contagious" and within the context of the mystico-religious game this statement might very well be true.

Perhaps the most powerful superstition of all is the golfer's fervent belief in the proverbial crock of gold at the end of the rainbow. Known as "The Golf Secret" it is an elixir of golfing perfection and a superstition that nets for the fortune-tellers of the Golf Game and their publishers hundreds of thousands of pounds annually.

Once again we turn from the landlubber to the aspiring seaman in the increasingly popular sport of yachting. It would be natural to expect to find some vestiges of nautical superstitions among the yachtsmen of our marinas and estuaries but while it is true that some of the older specialised beliefs of the sea have been adopted by the new urban community of yachtsmen the latter are infinitely less tradition-bound than one would have supposed. Certain time-honoured rites continue to be observed, like the champagne launching ceremony, and the occasional coin is still laid under the new mast for luck, a custom extending back to Roman times when it represented a symbolic sacrifice to the gods of the sea. This same custom takes place occasionally when a mast is lifted, at which time a piece of silver is left in its place until the following yachting season.

The lucky mascot is a fairly well established principle among yachtsmen, particularly the teddy bear, but as might be expected the individualistic type of luck-bringer tends to be replaced more and more by a St. Christopher medallion attached to the mast.

A number of curious superstitions which are still current among East Anglian yachtsmen and boat builders are without doubt survivals of maritime superstitions belonging to another age. A small coin is still occasionally thrown into the water during a storm, this being a form of sacrifice to the gods of the sea, although its original meaning has long been forgotten, and there appears to be a general acceptance of the concept of the jinxed boat. Green is still unpopular in a few places and is thought to bring disaster upon the owner of a boat of this colour. An expected relic of an ancient Viking ritual is represented by the custom, not yet extinct, in which a yacht is towed out to sea and either sunk or burned after the death of the owner. Usually it is only the wealthy yachtsman who can afford the luxury of this superstition, but when it takes place it is customary to preserve a rudder cap and sometimes the mast as a souvenir, the latter frequently serving as a flagpole ashore. *Britannia*, the flagship of King George V was apparently taken into the English Channel and sunk in deference to the tradition.

As a variant of this strange rite which is based upon the kinship between the ship-owner and his craft there is a custom in which the

ashes of the late owner are scattered over the water where he once
rode the tides and where the ship he loved so well in his lifetime had
been berthed.

Angling as a sport has inherited many superstitious attitudes from
life at sea and has acquired a number of others during its long
history as a sport. No doubt old Izaak Walton would have felt it
extremely unwise to ask a fisherman how many fish he had caught
so far for to answer such a question, as every angler knows, is
calculated to kill a day's fishing stone dead. Placing one's keep-net in
the water before catching one's first fish also tempts Providence,
since this is the equivalent of singing before breakfast or counting
one's chickens before they are hatched. Children fishing for stickle-
backs in ponds have inherited this fear of presuming upon the
future and hold it unlucky to fill their jam jars until the first fish has
been caught.

Fishing is essentially a game of chance, a venture into the
unknown and therefore an ideal crucible for the creation of private
forms of magic. Many anglers insist upon using the same float for
years on end or refuse to exchange one rod for another while
actually fishing, acting upon the principle that changing the method
changes the luck. As an additional lure to the unsuspecting fish the
bait is often spat upon before being cast into the waters. In common
with many deep-sea fishermen, inshore anglers consider it most
unlucky to utilise an upturned bucket as a seat.

Many anglers often accept some of the old fishermen's myths
handed down from medieval times as scientific facts. One is the
story that, however badly injured an eel might be, it is impossible
for it to die before sundown, which arises from the tradition that all
serpentine creatures were originally sun symbols, and that, the tench
is the "doctor fish" against whose greasy sides the other fish rub
themselves when sick and are thus cured.

Blood sports as one would expect incorporate a number of barbaric
survivals including the blooding of the young huntsman with the gore
of the newly-killed fox, otter or stag as an initiatory rite, the latter
having its hooves and heart removed, all of which are derived from
the hunting magic of the remote past. A form of blooding exists
among wildfowlers after the initiate has killed his first game bird. In
the United States the claw of the first bird shot is often adopted for an
amulet. Some hunters believe it not only dangerous but unlucky to
load their weapons before actually reaching the field.

To turn to some indoor sports might appear something of an

anticlimax, yet even the most unlikely recreational activity possesses its superstitions. A billiards player will often believe fervently in the power of a lucky cue. The late Joe Davis used one such cue continuously. Highly individual ritual movements are integral in billiard-table magic. A player will hold his cue in one particular position believing that any change or release of grip must adversely affect the shot that follows and bring a lucky break to an end. Boxers as far as superstitions are concerned seem to concentrate on lucky clothing. An old robe will often be treasured for years on end as a lucky charm.

Even the humble game of darts provides a field for ritualistic behaviour. Dart players generally consider it unlucky to play against a woman and will often perform some magical act prior to casting their dart. One player may touch the curtain for luck while another thrusts his left foot forward moving it from left to right as if to kick away some invisible obstacle standing between himself and the target.

The current bingo craze which has wrecked the domestic economy of many a household provides a first-class area for the study of superstitious beliefs in an entirely modern setting. Bingo players as a class are fervent believers in the power of lucky charms but even more in the power of a so-called "lucky" seat in the bingo hall.

The gambling fever, the pursuit of gain and the brooding fear of loss all intensify the emotions to fever pitch in all games of chance. This is very evident in card gambling for the act of playing cards has inherited from the pre-Christian past definite magical associations which were in all probability transmitted to them from their predecessors, the Tarot cards of the fortune teller. Our Puritan ancestors seem to have been well aware of this pagan aspect and it was not for nothing that cards were long known as "The Devil's Picture Books". In European folklore it was a common belief that the Devil always hid himself beneath the table during a game of cards and in the British Isles there are many legends in which the handsome stranger who lures the thoughtless youth into a card game on a Sunday is later discovered to be cloven-hoofed. Among certain classes of workers whose lives were always in danger, a pack of playing cards was once considered to be a bad luck-bringer and no miner would risk taking a pack into a mine, nor a fisherman aboard his boat, nor would a thief risk stealing a pack since this to his mind almost guaranteed that he would be caught.

Associated with the game of cards are many of the older types of superstition quite apart from those peculiar to card playing itself. To meet a woman on the way to a game or to play with a cross-eyed man is highly ominous since the one is potentially a witch—and at the very least devitalises the luck—while the other most likely has the evil eye. When cutting the cards one must never cut cross-wise as this symbolically "cuts the luck" while to drop a card during the game symbolises somewhat obviously perhaps, a fall in one's fortunes. It is a common custom when troubled with a phase of bad luck for a player to change seats or to call for a new pack, apparently from the belief that by changing either his position at the table or the cards he can also change his luck. And there are some players who attempt to defeat bad luck by standing up and encircling their chairs from left to right, this being the way of the sun, unconsciously following an ancient rite for bringing the sun's blessing upon an enterprise but it is also said to effectively isolate the bad luck by encircling it. On the other hand others will twist the chair while not moving from their own position. It is common also for a loser to place a handkerchief upon his seat and then to sit upon it, thus ritually providing himself with a new basis of operations and therefore a fresh start.

Forms of psychic defence used for protection against the demons of misfortune at cards can even involve in extreme cases carrying a badger's foot in the right hand jacket pocket. Of the innumerable other superstitions of card players perhaps the most revealing is the very common custom of attempting to cast a spell upon one's opponent by a ritual known as "crossing out the luck". To "cross out" the luck of another at the table one surreptitiously places a used matchstick in the ashtray and then equally unobtrusively places another crosswise upon it. Some gamblers are well aware of this device and with equal cunning will casually displace the crossed matches with a cigarette end. So strong is the fear of having one's luck accidentally "crossed out" that many gamblers carefully avoid playing against the grain of a wooden table. In Bridge a black ace that falls to the floor during a game is a sign to stop playing. It has also been noted that to play a private match after a bridge championship is unlucky.

In the past many games of chance were employed to divine the future, and included spinning a wheel or even a knife and deciding from the way it pointed what one's fate might be. To meet a woman on the way to a magic wheel was always a sign of ill-fortune and even today to come upon a lady en route to the roulette tables is just as ill-omened. Oddly enough play will always be lucky if it follows a suicide which doubtless symbolises a human sacrifice to Lady Luck. Gamblers carry to the roulette table all kinds of magical aids (to quote Gerald McKnight's *The Complete Gambler*) including : ". . . pieces of bone, skulls, claws, hooves, religious 'holy' mementoes, as well as Black Magic articles". Other luck-bringers include the human mascot, which in the United States is the pretty girl companion, although whether it is permissible to touch this kind of charm for luck is an open question !

The gambler who plays his hunch is probably unaware that the term itself originates from the supposed luck-bringing properties of the hunchback, a superstition that goes back to the grotesque dwarf god Bes of ancient Egypt, whose amulet is still worn in the Mediterranean area as protection against the evil eye. So strong is this superstition at Monte Carlo that more than one hunchback has obtained his living by selling to gamblers the privilege of touching his hump. Far better known, of course, is the story of the casino owner who employed a hunchback to hover in the vicinity of those who had won large sums of money at the tables as an inducement to them not to depart with their winnings but to try their luck again, with the result that the money invariably found its way back into the hands of the establishment.

The highly-charged emotional atmosphere of the gambling salon has an effect upon some players somewhat reminiscent of a seance. In this curious climate, almost entirely removed from the moral restraints and conventions of the day-to-day bourgeois world, the gambler is exposed to forces that seem infinitely stronger than his capacity to withstand them, and he is thrust, temporarily at least, back into the Stone Age. Beginner's luck is proverbial among gamblers and it is based upon the savage's superstitious awe of the magic of new things, in this case the new player.

The winning player will also discover that in most forms of gambling others at the table will begin to imitate his every gesture and mannerism as if by scratching the nose with the right hand or pursing the lips one exerted some secret power of command over the gods of fate. In many ways the gambler in following his "hunch" plays not so much with his money as with his soul, and the contest becomes in effect a ritual conflict, the penalty for the loser being almost a form of emotional death. In gambling, as in golf, the player, without realising it, plays against himself.

A very similar situation applies in the game of dice, which

evolved from an ancient divinatory rite with knuckle-bones to determine whether or not it was propitious for a tribe to go to war. The bones were later replaced by marked pebbles and were also used for fortune-telling. It is perhaps understandable that something of this old magic should have influenced the American crap-shooter's custom of making curious gestures with his hands when throwing his dice and snapping his fingers, a traditional method of driving away evil spirits. Other crap-shooters will even touch the more intimate parts of their bodies with the dice as if to endow the latter with procreative power. This last is curiously reminiscent of the rite of the old Icelanders in which a crushed raven's heart was rubbed upon the dice.

Gamblers observe many strict rules upon which they imagine the maintenance of good fortune to depend : they refuse to boast for this tempts Providence and they keep tight lips for silence is a retainer of power while speech expends it. Perhaps needless to say, it is considered unlucky for a gambler to burst into song. So valuable is this vital force called luck that the player must carefully insulate himself against incautiously transmitting it to another. For this reason no gambler will ever lend another gambler money as this symbolises disposing of some of his own luck. In this he merely follows the custom of fishermen who, for the same reason, refuse to lend any object from their boats.

There is possibly no department of human activity where the gambling spirit, tension and excitement are more dominant than in horse-racing, "the sport of kings". Horse-racing superstitions, broadly speaking, fall into three main groups : those relating to the horse itself, those associated with the jockey and, most important of all, those of the punter. It is traditional that the name of a horse, like that of a ship, must never be changed for this brings bad luck, nor must the animal be offered good wishes before the race begins. Owners who wish to be properly insured with the gods of chance will never boast, for reasons that will by now have become obvious, and their wives invariably wear new dresses before the race and often carry little amulets or charms in their handbags.

Jockeys as a class are extremely superstitious, and understandably find it necessary to maintain the strictest secrecy regarding their individual luck-bringing magic. They act no doubt upon the principle that talking about a luck secret diminishes its potency. As one would expect, many jockeys' superstitions involve clothing. A jockey will usually wear his "lucky suit" when he leaves home on the day of the race and when changing into his racing colours will be careful never to stand his riding boots on the floor, presumably because this act is symbolical of being unhorsed.

The emotional state of the betting man at the races brings into play the whole range of superstitions. Here, as perhaps nowhere else, the forces of "good" and "evil" stand poised for defence and attack. A man can be so disturbed at meeting a cross-eyed woman on the way to the course, since this apparently crosses out his luck, that he finds it necessary to counter the danger and restore the situation by crossing the road. In laying his bet a betting man will rarely reveal his choice of a horse to another, since this apparently reduces the prospects of winning. Incidentally a punter who selects his favourite by means of a pin is supposed to do much better should the pin have been first used on a wedding-dress, as this possesses a strong kind of magic. Horse-racing magic of course involves all the more familiar types of superstition : the lucky coin, the lucky colour or number and the mascot, although today's backers are less inclined than the sportsmen of a hundred years ago to display openly a lucky doll attached to their headgear. Any action or mannerism that has previously been followed by a win can, to the punter's mind, provide the basis for a superstition. A man whose horse happens to win after he has lit a cigarette, for example, will be inclined to repeat the same action before the next race.

One of the most incredible of the fetishes still occasionally met with among racegoers is the frog's bone mascot carried in the pocket. Until a century or so ago the belief still lingered in the countryside that one could obtain power over a horse by scattering a powder made from the bones of a toad or frog. Despite the decline in country witchcraft the old superstition has apparently never died out and has persisted in the form of a lucky charm in the sport of kings.

Sometimes a horse-racing superstition can spring out of the ground as it were, as in the case reported in the newspapers several years ago in which a clergyman decided to augment the church funds by betting on horses. He chose for his advisers an all-female committee and from their successes decided that, contrary to general belief, women were luckier in the betting game than men.

Even more prone to superstition than horse-racing is the theatre, both professional and amateur, which possesses all the elements necessary for the development and maintenance of superstitious attitudes. The play not only involves an inter-relationship between performer and onlooker but it is also a gamble, and this together with its long historical continuity renders it a potent agency for the transmission of magical beliefs from the past to the present. It is for this reason that many actors' superstitions tend to be stylised and are somewhat more familiar than those of other professions or activities.

An actor, like a gambler, creates his own superstitious fetishes based upon previous experience and, for this reason, the lucky charm or the lucky coin, which has become associated in his mind with some early success, will continue to play an important role as a luck-bringer. In the theatre, each actor is an individual standing alone and his choice of luck symbols tends to be extremely individualistic and not always recognisable to others. One actor likes to wash his hands with lucky soap, the soap belonging to a lucky fellow actor. Another will chant the jingle that he heard in his first play, or an actress will continue to wear a particular article of stage jewellery throughout her theatrical career. Singer Frankie Vaughan is said never to travel without his lucky silver-knobbed cane, while the American actor Glenn Ford always wore as his mascot the blue and red necktie purchased with his first pay packet as a juvenile lead. Some actors invariably proceed to and from the theatre by the same route, never risking the slightest variation. Some swear by human mascots, a well known example being the famous comedian Robertson Hare, who is considered a lucky man to work with.

Dressing room fetishism is very strong among both amateur and professional actors and reflects the principles found in other hazardous enterprises like mining and the seafaring. Whistling was originally forbidden because it had the power to "whistle up" an adverse wind (the failure of the play) a rite practised in the seventeenth-century by malevolent witches. Today it merely brings bad luck. The evil effect may be neutralised, however, if the whistler leaves the dressing room at once and turns round three times from left to right (the sunwise turn) before re-entering. Swearing vilely apparently also cancels the ill-effects. It is most unlucky for one actor to peer over the shoulder of a fellow actor who is looking into a mirror so that the two reflections appear together, this being without doubt a relic of the old fear of being overlooked by the evil eye. Shoes must never be placed on the dressing table as this brings bad luck both to the player and the production in the same way that it was once supposed to bring death to the householder.

The extreme economic hazards to which the strolling player was always subject is responsible for all kinds of surviving minor fetishes.

Crossed knives mean crossed lives and are symbols of psychic conflict.

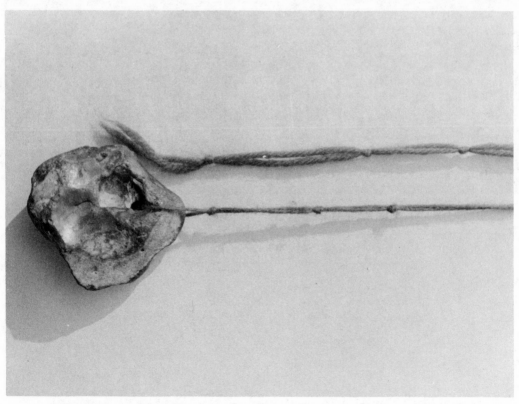

A hagstone rudely carved in the shape of a pentacle was once used to keep witches at bay.

In water divination black bubbles mean bad luck.

It is still said, for example, that the actor standing nearest the dressing room exit is most likely to be first to have to make an exit from his job.

Very few actors will tolerate a perfect rehearsal, believing this to be an open invitation to misfortune and for this reason the last, or "tag", line is never spoken. This superstition is of the same order as that of the old time bricklayer who refused to lay the last brick, and belongs to a group of superstitions associated with the fear of completing any process, as this is calculated to provoke the gods into hostile reactions. The cat, the embodiment of malevolent powers, although generally lucky among actors, is unwelcome at rehearsals since its presence there lets loose all the forces of hostile magic.

It is unlucky to peer at the audience through the wrong side of the curtain and for this reason there is a peep hole in the curtain, otherwise it would symbolise "curtains" for the production. Few actors, however kindly their natures, will wish good luck to a fellow actor before going on stage as this represents the transfer of some of their own store of good fortune to another. One recognises here the same fear, already mentioned, as that of the gambler who refuses to lend money to another gambler, and the fisherman's strong objection to the loan of any object from one fishing craft to another.

Actors are generally averse to receiving any form of congratulation since the act of drawing the attention of the gods to a success, invites their hostile intervention. Oddly enough many television actors go out of their way to defy theatre superstitions, and at one studio it is the firm rule that "good luck" be offered to everyone as they go on stage. The actor who has suffered the misfortune of being blessed prior to going on stage will be careful to offset the danger by muttering the words "Break a leg" or by emitting a stream of fearsome four-letter words. Actors also avoid discussing their luck since this, like the blessing, invites its opposite. Stumbling when going on stage is as ominous as it is to turn the handle of the wrong door when looking for the manager's office for it symbolises a bad start. Psychologically of course to stumble provides a fairly definite signal of temporary emotional instability.

On stage the colour green is considered unlucky as is occasionally yellow, the latter being the colour of the clothing worn by Satan in the old mystery plays. On the other hand a first night good luck telegram that shows signs of yellowing is a happy sign, most actors believing "the yellower the telegram the longer the run".

Knitting is frowned upon on stage since it is supposed to "knot" or entangle the production, perhaps harking back to the supposed power of the witch to "tie up" any process by symbolically knotting a piece of string or rope.

Certain plays have long been associated with bad luck from their inherent characteristics and also because of misfortunes that have followed their production. "Macbeth" as a play involving witchcraft becomes necessarily the focal point for terrors transmitted down the centuries from Shakespeare's time when witches were regarded as very real. It is not generally known that this play once contained a witches' dance. The witches' song is only safe if sung on stage, being then a form of play-acting; off-stage in a real life setting, however, it has the potency of a real curse. There is a studied reluctance among actors to refer to the play "Macbeth" by name, for even to utter the fatal word has been known to endanger a production, instead many actors use the euphemism "that play". Shakespeare is almost a totem figure among actors and any diminution in his stature is akin to the defilement of a god and therefore unlucky. For this reason Shakespeare's works must not be parodied and an attempt to set the bard to rock and roll once resulted in catastrophe.

There are curious relics of superstitious belief in the pantomime. The good fairy makes her entry on the right side of the stage and the evil one on the left, or sinister side, facing the audience. The pantomimes "Robin Hood" and "The Babes in the Wood" are supposed to be unlucky, yet "Cinderella" on the other hand is a lucky play.

In the theatre auditorium and box office a number of traditional superstitions are still well entrenched. It is still believed that if the first person to purchase a ticket on the first night happens to be elderly the play is destined to have a long run, but should he be young the run of the play will be correspondingly short. The first tip received by the programme seller on the first night is equally significant to the play's prospects and must be rubbed against the leg, not only to ensure a long run but as a guarantee that it will be followed by many more.

The range covered by the superstitions of the theatrical world is vast and inevitably extends into every other aspect of the entertainment industry including the circus and the television studio. There have been certain modifications over the years of course, and the time has probably passed when an acrobat preparatory to commencing his act would throw his cuffs on to the stage and decide if they remained fastened that the omen was good and that if they fell apart so would his performance, but this does not suggest that an acrobat is any the less superstitious but rather that detachable shirt cuffs are out of fashion. Ballerinas have their lucky powder puffs and specialised ways of wishing one another good luck. Singers regard particular songs as unlucky, including Tosti's "Goodbye", since this obviously portends a separation between the entertainer and his job, and "I dream't that I dwelt in marble halls", perhaps because of its suggestion of either the tomb or Paradise. Some musicians apparently regard it as highly dangerous to accept their pay cheque in advance of the performance since, by presuming upon the future, they thereby tempt fate into its usual reprisals. Others consider it unlucky to be interrupted while a piece is being played. Chorus girls and dancers will often preserve the heel of a dancing shoe as a lucky charm, declaring it to be worth its weight in gold.

The theatre is in effect an alchemist's laboratory for the transmutation of personality through acting, a stupendous exercise in imitative magic in which the performer becomes involved in a ritual drama conducted on more than one plane with emotional experiences of an almost supernatural character. Yet even so it is sometimes soul-shattering to discover the true depths of the supernatural beliefs and feelings of certain players. In one case, to the author's knowledge, a disgruntled actor wrote the name of a theatre manager whom he hated upon a piece of paper which he then burnt. Twice he did this—and twice his enemy got the sack. Obviously, in the theatre if nowhere else black magic sometimes works!

CHAPTER V

THE GRAND PROCESSION

LIFE can be compared in some ways to a grand procession which parades along a high road to vanish eventually into that dark tunnel we call death. To extend the metaphor even further, it is a route set with ceremonial arches each of which constitutes a ritual gateway separating past from future and symbolising renewal and re-birth. In primitive communities the transition from one phase of existence to another was always considered a highly dangerous process and therefore became the occasion for magical rites of a protective character. At such times the person concerned was considered to be very vulnerable to the assaults of evil spirits; hence the rigid observances associated with birth, puberty, marriage and death which have descended to us in the form of superstitions.

In view of what we know about the mind it is obvious that drastic changes in sequence can create points of tension which almost literally demand the creation of the protective wall of ritual. The social revolution of the nineteenth and twentieth centuries has done a good deal to modify the pressures in our lives with the result that superstitious attitudes have often retreated from one point of tension to another without actually vanishing from the scene.

Of necessity any study of this particular aspect of human behaviour must begin with the superstitions of birth. This, the primary phase or ceremonial entry into life, was medically speaking until very recently a phase of extreme vulnerability for both mother and child. Fear of the evil eye was universal at such a time and is hardly extinct today. In the Near East, for example, for anyone to praise a baby's beauty is most dangerous and worse than an insult. With the advent of safer motherhood, however, the vast bulk of old wives' lore has virtually disappeared, the superstitions that survive being concentrated in the main about the one principal element of uncertainty associated with birth—the sex of the expected child. This will often result in some amazing mental manoeuvres by those whose underlying belief in magic now comes to the fore. One mother will studiously wish with all her mind for the very opposite of her desires, creating the mental picture of a boy when she wants a girl. With another the magic is of a more direct character and specially chosen colours are worn by the mother-to-be during her pregnancy : blue if she desires a boy and pink if a girl. While few people today seriously believe that the state of mind of the mother can influence the physical appearance of the unborn child, as for example that the glimpse of a hare will result in the birth of a baby with a hare-lip, updated variations in the same theme are not at all uncommon. A novel example is the belief that a pregnant woman who reads scholarly books will produce a scholarly child. Another superstition, which is apparently vaguely associated with sunworship, holds that copulation should be restricted to high noon since conception must occur when the sun is at its zenith if a healthy child is to be born.

There still persists incredible as it may seem the curious fear that if a mother-to-be while bathing inadvertently swallows the egg of an octopus (an unlikely contingency in the British Isles) the egg will hatch out in the womb. This is without doubt the last relic of the ancient myth that a woman could conceive from a lower animal.

By anticipating a birth with too great a confidence a woman tempts Providence, and for this reason very few will actually take delivery of the perambulator at the house before the baby is born.

Very prevalent also is the belief that an affinity between mother and son is established in the womb, and this finds expression in many curious experiences similar to what is now more commonly described as extra sensory perception. It is an unquestioned fact, however, that some mothers are convinced that there exists an avenue of communication between mother and son that continues throughout life.

The actual moment of birth is often considered to have a distinct bearing upon a child's psychic powers. Babies born at the "chimes hours", that is three, six, nine and twelve o'clock, are supposed to be blessed with second sight, and are credited with the power to see ghosts. A Sunday's child is proverbially not only lucky but gifted. However, it is most unlucky to be born at ebb tide and even more so to have a set of teeth at birth as this means that one is likely to become a murderer. The reason for this is obvious. Teeth were our primary weapons and hence became symbols of aggression.

The old belief that a mother remained unclean following the birth of her child until she had been ritually cleansed or churched, is still tenaciously adhered to in some working-class communities.

Even where the full force of the superstition is in decline, a visit to relatives by an unchurched mother with her baby is unlucky. In a more recent variant of the same superstition a married couple visited by an unchurched mother can expect to have a new baby of their own whether they like it or not.

The old superstition that a child must go up in the world before it goes down was observed in the past by the father carrying the new baby in his arms to the top of the stairs and then descending them again, but in its latest version the flat dweller ceremoniously mounts a step-ladder instead. The rites of the newborn can take very strange forms in a community that has been little touched by change. The author was recently told that in a remote Scottish village community it is customary for the mother to take her new baby to the seashore, and there to dip her finger in sea-water with which she then marks its shoulder, thereby making it "a son of the sea".

The choice of a name for a child is still a matter of great importance from the standpoint of superstition. The names of the fortunate are readily adopted, but those associated with tragedy speedily go out of fashion. Among primitive people in the past the name was so integral a part of the personality that it was often kept secret out of fear that anyone who learned it would have the power to work witchcraft against its owner. The first haircut is also associated with curious rituals the world over, the child's short tresses being retained by the mother as a kind of souvenir. The child's first tooth extraction is also accompanied by ritual play-acting in which the molar is purchased for sixpence and placed under the pillow for the fairies to take away. Originally it would have been preserved in order to be placed in the coffin at death so that the body would be physically complete on Judgment Day.

The child's first birthday is invariably accompanied by the ceremonial lighting of a single candle to bring it good fortune, this being a relic of the sacred fires lit in ancient Greece in honour of the birthday of Artemis, goddess of the moon, and patroness of marriage and childbirth at which time moon-shaped cakes with tapers were placed upon the altars in the temples. The German peasants invariably lit candles on a cake when the child first awoke on its birthday. The pleasing custom of blowing out the candles with a single puff in order to make a wish come true was originally a rite to gain the favour of Artemis.

Even the bells attached to a baby's harness or to the

perambulator were originally protective devices based on the belief that the ringing of bells frightens off evil spirits. The coloured balls we see attached to the baby's cot were once intended as magic charms to ward off the evil eye from the cradle.

Children, especially younger ones, are naturally predisposed to the belief in magic, the outward trappings of which tend to be discarded as they grow older. The child accepts as real, magical creatures which populate a make believe world and it seems perfectly natural to it that animals should possess quasi-human powers. This almost animistic approach overlaps into later childhood when the "lucky" charms of children will often be toy animals, dogs, cats, even plastic elephants. The superstitions of the older child and especially the teenager sometimes tend to take on a somewhat more sombre note. Collected in one day from children of an East London school were the following gems of magical lore, which would seem to suggest an unsuspected preoccupation with the macabre among the young:

Never wear a brown and a black shoe lace at the same time for brown means graveyard earth, and black death.

It is bad luck to put on a cardigan inside out. To offset the danger one must turn in a complete circle three times.

If you wish to do harm to another child stare hard at the nape of its neck and wish hard. Incidentally good fortune can be transmitted by precisely the same process.

If you stumble while ascending the stairs the one immediately behind you will die.

If there are three knocks on the window—expect a death.

To dream of teeth means a death in the family.

The ghostly beliefs of the young are so profuse and in such variety that to incorporate them in detail would be an impossibility. Integral in the ghost lore of teenage girls, however, is one constant theme—terror of a phantom emerging from a wardrobe or cupboard in the bedroom, and then standing at the foot of the bed, a superstition confined entirely it would appear to the female of the species, and no doubt symbolising a sublimated fear of rape.

If there is any area of activity where superstition retains its strongest hold among those passing through or beyond the transition stage of puberty it is in the realm of sex. For untold centuries old wives' tales have been handed down from one generation to the next usually in the form of whispered advice from mother to

daughter or as a part of the erotic folklore of youth. The puritan-
ical climate in which sex was a tabooed subject was ideal for the
preservation of the older sexual myths and even now in spite of
more open discussion of the sexual act and the greater availability
of educational literature a good many of the old illusions persist.
The superstitions of puberty include many relics of completely
outmoded magical concepts all of which must have been handed
down from ancient time to form part of the folklore of sexual
life.

In L. T. Woodward's interesting handbook *90% of What you
Know about Sex is Wrong*, may be found many amazing superstitions which are usually classed as simple misinformation, virility
as one might expect being a subject well to the fore. The ancient
association of male sexual potency with the generative power of
the sun is responsible for the age old myth that Latins and dark
men generally, especially those originating from lands where the
sun is hot, are more passionate than fair ones. The latest manifestation of this intriguing myth takes the form of the belief that a
course of sun-lamp treatment will stimulate the male sex drive.

Because it was once assumed that the vital properties contained
in the human hair were responsible for sexual energy, we have the
modern myth that scanty bodily hair is a sign of lack of virility,
whereas in actual fact precisely the opposite pertains.

The traditional belief that innate qualities are invariably
betrayed by some external sign provided by nature, is responsible
for the superstition widespread among the younger generation in
America and the British Isles that men with large hands and feet
possess large sexual organs, and that a woman with a generous
mouth has a large vagina. Even more deeply entrenched is the
venerable fallacy that spicy foods make good aphrodisiacs. Fish,
because of its prolific egg-laying powers, is at the top of the
traditional list of love foods. In this connection it is perhaps not
too surprising to discover that a special cookbook has now been
published in America designed "to draw lovers together". At the
present time in the West of England there is a rapidly developing
myth that watercress encourages fertility.

A number of surviving prohibitions reflect the medieval attitude
to sex as a sinful and therefore dangerous pursuit; for example
that overmuch sexual intercourse weakens the heart and causes
blindness, and that the wedding ceremony confers immunity to
venereal disease. Perhaps the most long-standing of all the old

social myths is the once officially fostered illusion that masturbation is somehow harmful to the individual.

While it is true that most of these myths have arisen from sheer misinformation or from garbled knowledge passed on from one teenager to another, even the latest scientific developments in sexual knowledge have a tendency to become bogged down in mythology. Among many young people any pill, even an aspirin, becomes an acceptable oral contraceptive, while as indicated in a recent family planning publication a do it yourself type of magical birth control involves jumping up and down after intercourse to avoid pregnancy. The very latest, and perhaps most eccentric of superstitions is that a woman with contact lenses is unable to take the oral contraceptive pill.

Love charms of a purely magical character may still be found in the teenage repository of amatory superstitions, but whereas the English country wench of long ago placed a leaf in her shoe to lure her suitor the young American equivalent places a drinking straw in her shoe instead. However there is now available a special lucky charm that guarantees success in love. It is extremely hazardous to the prospects of any permanent union for a girl to knit a sweater for her boyfriend since by anticipating the functions of a housewife she presumes upon Providence which can be expected to come down with a heavy hand upon all invasion of its territorial rights.

If the rites of courtship today have been reduced to little more than an invitation to bed the same cannot be said for marriage which, for the vast majority of women, retains its sacred qualities undiminished by the iconoclasm of a permissive society. It is possibly due to the fact that marriage still embodies such a vast element of superstition that the ceremony has managed to survive more or less intact. Every aspect of the approach to marriage is of the utmost psychic importance; every rite retains much of its original magical potency. At this momentous time when magic is in the air if the engagement ring should happen to break or be lost it indicates a possible termination of the engagement, and of course every stone in the ring has its important symbolic association. Birthstones might today be less popular than in the past but the diamond still remains the greatest favourite, symbolising constancy, indestructibility, joy and love.

The choice of the wedding date in most cases still precludes the month of May which has been unlucky for marriages for centuries, a superstition arising almost certainly from the fact that May was the month dedicated by the ancient Romans to their family dead, and was even in ancient times considered unlucky for lovers.

The ceremony of marriage itself is particularly important from the standpoint of superstition in that it represents one of the last surviving *rites de passage* from one state of existence to another. It is surrounded with taboos which must be observed to the letter, as it is a psychically dangerous time with demonic forces threatening the young couple. The bride must not be seen by the groom in her wedding dress prior to the ceremony nor must she look at herself in the mirror once she has been completely dressed for it is dangerous to anticipate the future by projecting her image as a married woman into the glass. Brides who risk that last peep at their reflections are careful to leave the dress incomplete in some way, and will often delay picking up their gloves until after looking in the mirror. Once again one discovers this same inner fear of completing any process whether it be related to a building, the rehearsal of a play or a wedding dress. As for the wedding dress and veil, these are surrounded with the strangest rites. The veil is a relic of the seclusion in which the prospective bride was kept in ancient times as it was then thought that if she were seen she could do psychic injury to her neighbours and family, not to mention her husband-to-be. It also had a secondary purpose in protecting the bride from the dangers of the evil eye of jealous rivals and spinsters. The colours of the wedding dress have still to be chosen with care if the fate of the marriage is not to be prejudiced in advance. "Marry in red wish you were dead" has a very clear-cut association with the sins of the scarlet woman of the Bible.

The curious superstition that a bride will be lucky if her wedding dress contains "something old, something new, something borrowed and something blue" is based upon the importance of maintaining links with the past (old), the future (new), and borrowed (the present), while blue since the times of the ancient Israelites has always represented purity. Incidentally the working girl who inserts the first stitch in the wedding dress can expect to be married herself before the year is out, such is the luck-bringing property of this magical garment.

For the wedding car to break down *en route* to the church is extremely unlucky, being perhaps ominous of a breakdown of the marriage, while the gold wedding ring, a circle symbolising the unity of the bond of matrimony, must never be removed for if it is lost or is broken the marriage will suffer a similar fate.

Flowers at a wedding symbolise fertility, in particular orange blossoms which were originally introduced from the Near East by the Crusaders and which were used for centuries as love charms and also provided magical protection against barrenness. At the wedding of Jackie Kennedy to Aristotle Onassis in Greece in 1968 the newly married couple, after dancing slowly around the altar, were crowned with orange blossoms. Flowers worn by the grooms- men in their buttonholes are symbols of the ribands worn in Anglo-Saxon times as marriage knots and represent the "bonds" of marriage.

The custom of sending a piece of wedding cake to absent members of the family and friends is a historically modern deve- lopment of a very ancient custom. In the past the wedding cake ensured that the marriage would be successful and today each recipient of a portion of cake shares in the luck of the bride. Confetti, a substitute for the rice and sweetmeats of an earlier period, is an emblem of fruitfulness, a magical protection against barrenness and, despite the prejudice of certain tidy-minded modern clergymen, is unlikely to go out of favour as long as the ceremony of marriage persists.

The bridal bouquet is an interesting example of a superstitious rite that has taken on a new form over the centuries. It was once the custom for the groomsmen to struggle for the bride's garter following the wedding, since possession of this article was supposed to bring good luck, but for reasons of decorum this was replaced by throwing the bouquet by the bride, a ritual which transferred the luck to the bridesmaid who caught it. A very curious survival relating to the custom in its original form recently came to light in a village in East Yorkshire where a necktie is given to every bachelor present at the wedding reception as a good-luck token.

No Roman wedding would have been complete without the presence of its clown to sing farcical songs containing obscenities which were specifically designed to avert from the newly married couple the jealousy of the gods or the evil eye of some envious guest. It is a curious fact of social behaviour that even today the proverbial funny man will inevitably be present at the wedding reception to provide his fellow guests with unasked-for entertainment in the form of crude jokes and obscene allusions.

If the honeymoon is a comparatively modern innovation in so far as it involves the happy couple taking a journey away from home, the use of the term is by no means so. Honey was an

A collection of schoolchildren's lucky mascots.

Messenger of fate. The cry of an owl—universally a foreboding of illness and death.

aphrodisiac and in northern Europe the wedding guests drank honey for a whole moon or month following the ceremony.

Carrying the bride over the doorstep into her new home originated with the necessity of avoiding the threatening evil spirits that gathered outside every threshold. There was also a secondary consideration in that it was considered inappropriate for a girl who was so soon to lose her virginity to profane with her touch the threshold that in Roman times had been dedicated to Vesta the Goddess of Virginity.

After her marriage, a woman enters into the primary phase of her existence, becoming in her own person a vehicle of transition, the initiator of new life and therefore a symbol of continuity. During this process she will often be conscious of strange emotions within herself, and may sometimes become prey to the strangest superstitions. Unlike the man, who moves on through the various stages of maturity with little outward impact upon his emotional life, the woman is in a state of continuous evolution as she passes through and beyond the ritual phases of marriage, childbirth and menopause. A surprising number of women subscribe consciously to the concept of the domestic elemental in that they believe that they have a protective spirit in the home which offers guidance in times of stress. Cases actually occur in which women claim to have seen such a presence, particularly during childbirth, although even then it is often in the form of a dream. A mother is sometimes conscious of the presence of her child although the two might be far apart, perceiving it in a flash of clairvoyant insight, or hearing her name called.

As the years pass, and most of life is left behind, one witnesses the final departure of many friends and relations. Death ceases to be a tiny dark figure upon the horizon; it grows larger, draws nearer. It is heard and sometimes sensed . . .

It is traditional in the lore of superstitions that death does not come without casting its shadow before, and into this category come the vivid experiences of men and women to whom the etheric double (or *Doppelgänger* of the Germans), so frequently reveals itself immediately prior to the time of passing. To the vast majority of humanity, however, premonition of death is limited to the unexpected shudder which is said to indicate that someone is walking over one's grave, a sure sign of the presence of the dark angel. However it is more often the voice of someone at the point of death that is heard and far less frequently nowadays than in the past, the traditional warning three knocks on the window pane. How one should classify the phenomena existing in that nether world between superstition and clairvoyance is difficult to say for to a considerable extent they belong equally to both categories.

It is perhaps only to be expected that the superstitions associated with the final exit should persist with much of their original vigour, for death remains an enigma, a state of complete loneliness and the only completely incommunicable experience undergone by man, as well as being the most fearful and at the same time most perfect of fulfilments. In the past however it was not customary to separate the idea of death from that of the passage of the soul into a new environment, for death was regarded as a new beginning, rather than an end. A number of the older death superstitions still survive, particularly in working-class districts, one of the best known being that the dead must never be left in the house unaccompanied by a living person. Originally this was supposed to protect the corpse from becoming the prey of demons. With the coming of death the windows are opened to facilitate the passage of the spirit, the blinds are drawn, the mirrors covered and a sackcloth-and-ashes psychology darkens the lives of those immediately involved. The mourner, as Geoffrey Gorer says in his *British Way of Death*, is now in a "special state of mind".

Despite the decline in the more strict type of funeral ceremony, much of the old type of superstition has managed to survive into our own iconoclastic age in the form of stylised rituals. Flowers were laid on the grave originally as a sacrifice of something living to buy happiness for the dead, but they are now placed there as a tribute of affection. The wreath was in ancient times a magic circle designed to enclose the soul of the dead and to prevent its return to haunt the living. Mourning dress was once the badge of spiritual contagion involving all those intimately connected with the deceased.

If we regard the ghost as an earthbound soul which cannot move on to the next phase of existence without the performance of certain obligatory ritual acts by those left behind in the realm of the living we shall have a far clearer understanding of the role of the funeral as a superstitious belief. Given that the funeral rites served to dispose of the dead at three levels—the physical, the spiritual and the psychological—we can now understand why any neglect of these rites was supposed to result in the return of an angry and menacing spirit determined to make life as troublesome as possible for its living relatives until the ceremonies of death had been properly observed. The funeral, therefore, fulfils in a somewhat dramatic manner the same function as that of knocking on wood, since it is intended not only to facilitate the departure of the spirit but to offset the dangers of its return. Any study of ghost lore indicates the reiteration of the same theme in popular belief. If the obligations to the dead or the funeral rites are neglected the dead, in the form of your conscience, can be expected to haunt you, and morbid imagination can be relied upon to do the rest. The heaviest load borne by guilt-ridden humanity is the secret satisfaction that the dead are dead. Ghost stories therefore tend to fall into a number of fairly clearly defined categories, all of course based upon the superstitious attitudes of the living towards the dead.

The brief anecdotes that follow were collected by the author during a tour of the country in the winter of 1967–8 and are representative of the basic themes underlying most ghostly phenomena, although some are admittedly of a somewhat mournful character :

The unfulfilled obligation to the dead. Bettiscombe Manor in Dorset has long been the proud possessor of a skull originally thought to have been that of a Negro male servant but later discovered to be that of a prehistoric woman. The Negro who was brought as a slave to Bettiscombe in the seventeenth century exacted from his master the promise that he would be returned to his native Africa for burial. Instead he was interred in the local churchyard where his ghost made its presence felt by screams and roars from the tomb. Finally the skeleton was transferred to Bettiscombe Manor where the skull still survives as a souvenir-cum-lucky-charm.

Murder and burial in unconsecrated ground. Reculver, site of the Roman fortress in Kent, was long reputed to be the scene of a haunting by a young child who, it was said, had been "buried alive by the Romans". In 1966 during excavations the skeletons of a number of babies were discovered interred at the corners of the various rooms, relics of human sacrifice carried out *circa* A.D. 400.

The suicide cannot rest. Wanstead Hospital in Essex was said to be haunted by the figure of a nun in grey. It now appears that towards the end of the last century a sister of mercy committed suicide on the premises and was afterwards buried in the grounds. Her ghost is occasionally seen today.

The traditional ancestral family ghost or banshee gives warning of death. An Accrington family always receives "notice" of a forthcoming death from a "faceless white thing" which materialises before the eyes of the horrified wife.

A spirit earthbound by love of the living. A mother who died in great anguish at leaving her children has often been seen hovering near their beds peering into their faces with an expression of infinite love.

From birth to death, we are surrounded by the most amazing superstitions, most of which defy interpretation. We can comprehend a little of their history and sometimes a clue to their meaning. We laugh at them, and defy them, but in the end we remain, like our ancestors, their helpless slaves.

CHAPTER VI

BODY AND CLOTHES

THE HUMAN BODY is taken so much for granted that its original role in magic and superstition is in some danger of becoming forgotten. To mystics of all ages, however, the body has always represented the temple of life to be preserved, honoured and, above all, protected like one's house and home against the invasion of hostile forces from outside. Primitive people appear to have taken up this position from the very earliest times and to have instituted complicated magical rites and ceremonies for the protection of the body against disease and death, for which they held attacking demons responsible. At a time in history when magic was the dominating factor only a fool would have disregarded its precepts, and it is for this reason that magical beliefs have to a diminishing extent continued to influence the reasoning of the vast majority of mankind until the present day.

Many examples of this pre-scientific approach to life have survived as health superstitions. One can still come upon such gems of obsolete anatomical lore as, for example, that the body completely renews itself every seven years and that the human eye emits a ray of light, but there exist also a surprising number of attitudes which would seem to represent more deeply rooted factors in the human psyche.

A fairly common example of this style of thinking is the superstition that should one feel particularly well it is a certain sign of forthcoming sickness. Another is that fear of a particular disease enhances the possibility of succumbing to it. Needless to say, the utterance of doom-laden, magically charged words like "death" or "cancer" is studiously avoided upon the principle: "Speak of the devil and he's sure to appear." A recent survey among young men revealed that what they feared most was cancer, impotence, paralysis and insanity, in that order.

The superstitions of medicine have declined in the main not so much because of the intellectual enlightenment of the community as a whole but rather because self medication is today out of fashion and that treatment lies in the hands of scientifically trained doctors. In those cases where the layman follows his inclination, however, he is quite likely to choose as his medical adviser one of the modern fringe medicine men, or even a psychic healer. Even now a good deal of the prestige enjoyed by professional doctors and surgeons is derived as much from the awe they excite in their patients as from their particular skills which, of course, lie completely beyond the comprehension of the layman. Even so, it is somewhat surprising to discover that when mankind still chooses to treat its own diseases it resorts to the most primitive health superstitions, most of which have been handed down from our barbaric past. Belief in magical medicine is by no means confined to the poor, and the following examples collected by the author from middle-class housewives in the north of England will make this clear.

To ease a burnt finger place the whole hand near the fire; this relieves the pain by distributing it over a wider area. An earlier generation of old wives might have carried out this remedy on the principle that like cures like, one of the fundamental rules of primitive magical healing.

To cure cramp place a magnet at the foot of the bed. The belief in the power of magnetism to draw a disease from the body by way of the extremities was one of the fetishes encouraged by magician healers, like Valentine Graterakes, the seventeenth-century seer, who was reputed to have pulled diseases out of the bodies of his "patients" by the laying-on of hands. Later still, in the early nineteenth century, the quack Perkins obtained great fame from his metallic tractors by means of which he claimed to extract from the ailing frame (to quote) "pains in the head, face, teeth, breast, stomach or back".

That measles can be transferred from one child to another by contagion, freeing the original sufferer from the disease at the same rate as a fellow mortal contracts it, is a superstition not at all uncommon in some parts of Devon, being based upon the ancient concept that sickness represents a form of diabolical possession and that the demon responsible can only be expelled from the body by transferring it to another abode, often a tree or an animal, but more frequently a human being.

That the forefinger of the right hand is the "poison" finger and must not be used to apply ointment to a wound as the latter will not then heal, is a European-wide superstition apparently based on the old fear of the "witch finger", the lethal pointing finger which a sorceress directed at her victim. The superstition is still strong in parts of Oxfordshire and in the north of England and apparently shows little signs of dying out.

Folk medicine, in so far as it belongs to the superstitions of healing, falls into two main categories : one relating to the laity and the other pertaining to its modern adepts, the flourishing school of fringe medicine men, some of whom have made miracle healing their profession. Much of fringe medicine belongs to the category of revival rather than survival, but it is nevertheless founded four-square upon the superstitions of sickness.

In the west of England the ringworm-charmer may still occasionally be found, usually curing by means of a handed-down system of mysterious passes and muttered charms. Wart-charmers are fairly common, however, for wart-charming is an art which the ordinary individual can practise without reference to the specialist. It would appear from the following examples collected by the author that this represents one of the oldest forms of magic. "Rub milkweed into the wart, then bury the milkweed and as it decays so will the wart" says one rustic soothsayer. "Notch a hazel stick, rub the notch into the wart and forget it. In nine days the wart will heal" says another. In some rural areas the wart is rubbed with the body of a snail which is then impaled on a thorn. For the success of this type of cure secrecy is imperative, for if the charm is ever revealed it loses its potency. Physicians will occasionally humour young children by purchasing their warts from them for sixpence, and they have even been known to ask the child to keep the matter a dead secret. An Essex charmer does not even require the physical presence of his patient but is content to make mysterious passes over a photograph of the wart in the privacy of his own home. The oddest superstition of this kind discovered so far, however, was the East Anglian cure : "Draw a chalk line inside the chimney and the wart will vanish at the same rate as the mark becomes obscured by the soot."

Superstitious practices of this kind are far more general in the British Isles than is popularly supposed. Perhaps the greatest myth of the scientific age is that superstitions can be ousted by science, whereas in fact they are either adapted and dished up in a pseudo scientific guise or temporarily driven underground. In one small Norfolk village a farm labourer's wife practises a little magical herbalism as a sideline by suspending her gold ring on a piece of thread above nine bottles of medicine. Directly the ring begins to turn

in a clockwise direction she serves the potion from the bottle immediately beneath it to her equally superstitious patient. In the late
sixteenth century it was just this type of healing that was denounced
as an example of the witchcraft then in vogue. Today of course
pendulum diagnosis has made a very fashionable comeback as one of
the techniques of fringe medicine and is used not only to determine
the sex of the unborn child but to diagnose heart disorders.
Archaeologists of the whimsical type have even been known to utilise
the technique to discover buried objects, and recently divination by
means of a needle suspended over a map brought to light a number of
skeletons on a medieval site near London. Even more eccentric,
however, was the recent advertisement offering miniature eucalyptus
trees for sale with supposedly "wonder properties" for staving off the
dangers of serious illness.

Despite the absence of the vampire from British folk life, the theme
occasionally crops up among the superstitions of medicine. Not at all
uncommon is the belief that certain individuals are unconsciously
psychic vampires, and that if allowed to sleep in the same room as
a sick person they will "draw off" his strength and thereby imperil his
recovery.

Far more widespread and strongly established, however, are the
many hospital superstitions that are accepted unquestioningly by
nurses and patients alike. Woe betide the good-hearted but unthink-
ing visitor who brings red and white flowers into the ward. Almost
certainly these will be discreetly removed, usually to the chapel,
perhaps appropriately since, as pointed out earlier, red and white
flowers were once associated with death for they were spread on the
graves of lovers by the ancient Romans. Yet another hospital superstition disguised as a scientific precaution is the practice of removing
flowers from the wards at night since it is supposed quite erroneously
that they exhaust the oxygen and are therefore harmful. This superstition has its roots in the ancient belief that flowers can be the homes
of evil spirits which emerge at night to injure the sick. Inspired by a
similar misconception, nurses will frequently close the ward windows
at night since night air is thought injurious but this too is based upon
the same type of forgotten superstition, i.e. that demons ventured
forth after dark to attack sleeping mankind. Another common
hospital superstition declares it to be most ominous if a patient up-
sets a chair, presumably because of a purely arbitrary association
of a falling chair with the final collapse of a patient.

The nurse who, while making the bed, unthinkingly places new blankets over a chair may anticipate three successive deaths in the ward. In this respect it should be remembered that in the past the dead were often wrapped in woollen blankets before burial, and of course as everyone knows "deaths always happen in threes". Saturday, according to an old superstition, is an unlucky day to move house since it is under the evil sign of Saturn, planet of death; from which it is but a step in logic to the modern hospital superstition that a patient discharged on a Saturday is destined to be readmitted to hospital very soon.

Few people realise that up to a century or so ago scientific medicine had not fully developed, and that ritualism played a considerable part in the relationship between doctor and patient. A surviving relic of the old-time pandering to the superstitious susceptibilities of the patient is illustrated by the colouring of pills. Black was studiously avoided as a pill colour because of its original association with death, while iron pills will often be red because of the association of this colour with blood in the patient's mind. Pink pills are often prescribed for girls whose physical development is retarded, "pink pills for pale people" being one of medicine's most famous maxims.

The superstitions of sickness are closely related to certain prevailing myths about mind and body which, despite scientific refutation, still maintain their hold in the second half of the twentieth century. The belief that lunacy is still regarded as a demonic disease somehow deserving of punishment was the conclusion of a writer in a recent article in the medical magazine *Pulse* in discussing the case of a magistrate who had been prepared to reduce the penalty for larceny provided the culprit consented to undergo pre-frontal leucotomy, which is obviously an attitude of mind reminiscent of the driving out of devils of madness by blows and other forms of cruelty as practised in medieval times.

A curious belief in the compensating power inherent in nature takes the form of the superstition that should an individual lose the use of a limb the other limbs will become correspondingly stronger, this being apparently a latter-day expression of the old doctrine that the body, as the temple of life, has the inherent power of self healing.

Blood is surrounded by many fetishist beliefs, based in the main upon the primitive doctrine that it was the vehicle of life containing soul power. One still occasionally hears it declared that the blood of the innocent cries out for revenge or that the blood of the murdered will indelibly stain the soil upon which it falls. Even more amazing are the powers ascribed to the human eye. It is often said that it is possible to make an individual turn his or her head by staring at the back of his neck, while to meet an individual with a squint is as unlucky today as it was in the past, when it was regarded as a sign of the evil eye. Eyebrows that meet across the nose are said to indicate a violent temper, this being a relic of the medieval superstition that "pagan eyes", as they were then called, were the hallmark of the witch. Among the Scots such an individual was supposed to be foredoomed to suffer a violent death. The superstition that the retinas of the eyes of a murdered person reveal a "photographic" image of the murderer is apparently only now becoming obsolete.

At this particular period in time when whole communities are split asunder on the subject of long hair as worn by men, it has become fashionable to equate length of locks with degeneracy—in complete defiance of the traditional and equally erroneous belief that human strength is bound up in the hair, the most obvious example being the Biblical Samson. A luxuriant head of hair was once taken as a token of virility, and the belief that now prevails is in effect merely a twentieth-century contradictory superstition which asks us to believe that the strength of the state and the stability of society generally is in some unexplained way dependent upon the length of hair worn by its citizens. Older attitudes often prevail, however, in the case of the disposal of shorn locks which many women still studiously burn in deference to the ancient superstition that by retaining cut hair one incurs the danger of sickness. In one such case to the author's knowledge it was only when the hair had been thrown into the fire that the sick person (a woman) claimed to have recovered her health. Hair superstitions of the most amazing kind still come to light. One is the belief that lost hair can be restored either by prayer or even by positive thinking. The association of hair with supernaturalism has recently been reinforced by a new cult based on astrology. One popular journal has even offered its readers a hair style inspired by the stars—which is described as a "hairoscope".

On the other hand the teeth, the first weapon of man for attack and defence, have lost almost all their traditional lore, due largely to the advance of dental science. The old superstition that a child born with teeth is destined to become an aggressive

Cat—symbol of mystery. To ill-treat any cat brings bad luck.

A symbolic destroyer of evil—a protector and luck-bringer.

This ambivalent amphibian brings both good and bad luck. Never kill a toad or a storm will surely follow.

character and even a murderer is referred to in Shakespeare's
Henry VI :

> The midwife wondered and the women cried
> Oh Jesus bless us, he is born with teeth.
> And so I was; which plainly signified
> That I should snarl and bite and play the dog.

The face, the façade of the personality, has always been one of
the focal points of superstition. Among surviving illusions of this
type may be found the belief that a noble brow is a sign of
intelligence, a long head an index of long-sightedness, a protruding
chin a sign of masculinity and strength whereas in fact the
mentally deficient have not infrequently possessed brows of greater
nobility than scholars. The prestige of the strong chin is based
upon the old superstition that a dominant or aggressive individual
is endowed with a protruding jaw. Facial superstitions have
acquired the status of an occult art in Hong Kong where face-
reading has become a profession, with lawyers and businessmen
among its clientele. Lawyers have always been a superstitious lot.
Up to seventy years ago they were always in the market for the
purchase of cauls, the possession of one of these being a guarantee
of eloquence. The Oriental face-reader warns his clients against
beak-nosed individuals since they obviously possess the instincts of
the predatory hawk, while an ape-like mouth is dismissed as a sign
of immaturity. In the West, however, the same superstition mani-
fests itself in less complicated ways. It is often taken for granted in
Britain that thin lips indicate meanness and thick ones passion and
sensuality.

The human hand, man's first tool, continues to be associated with
the older kind of superstitious belief. In Durham, for example, it is
still thought unlucky to meet a left-handed man on any day other
than a Tuesday, a superstition which is said to be connected with
the left-handed Scandinavian god Tiw after whom Tuesday was
named. The left or sinister side still retains its dark reputation, going
back to classical times and earlier when birds flying on the left were
considered inauspicious. If the left hand itches you will be giving
away money, while if the right hand itches you will receive money
instead. To cross a palm with silver remains even today the
prescribed method of paying the fortune-teller.

Crossing the fingers to offset the intrusion of unlucky forces has
obvious associations with the symbolism of the Cross, a sacred

symbol which has been revered from remotest antiquity. Children who say, "Cross my heart if I tell a lie. God will punish me when I die", bear testimony to the original supernatural power of the oath, the cross, and the heart as reinforcements of the given word in medieval times and earlier.

The old superstition which held that a child whose forefinger was longer than his second was destined to become a thief, is today represented by the belief that the fingers of anyone who takes up picking pockets as a profession will have a tendency to grow that way.

Contemporary finger-nail lore lays it down that one can foretell the future by examining the white spots on the nails. A black spot, it should be pointed out, is an unmistakable sign of death. Fear of cutting the nails on either a Sunday or a Friday remains one of our strongest superstitions, and is in all probability based on the taboo against violating the day of rest or working on the day of infamy.

Pointing has likewise long been a social taboo, originally because it was the means of casting an evil spell upon the one pointed at; while Churchill's two-finger sign, once a gesture of defiance against the evil eye, has now been reduced to a plebeian gesture of contempt. Many foot superstitions, some of a most bizarre character, have their dedicated devotees. It might be of comfort to those born with an extra toe to know that they are destined to be lucky in life, while as every Scotswoman is aware a man with a second toe longer than his great toe makes an ill-natured husband. Like the face and hands, the feet have recently been elevated into a contemporary superstitious cult, for it appears that footprint reading has become a branch of clairvoyance. To complete this mysterious saga of the foot one should note that the custom in which shoe salesmen try on the right shoe before the left, whatever its practical purpose, is one of the more unexpected relics of the old superstition that for luck one must always avoid the left side which is where the devil stands.

In many ways our clothing superstitions are simply extensions of the older lore associated with the human body, and there is good reason for the belief that in warmer climes at least dress was adopted originally for ritual purposes and that apart from ceremonial occasions nakedness or near nakedness was once the rule. Clothing in particular derived much of its occult properties as the direct result of its tactile relationship with the body and in the past was supposed to be endowed with a distinct magical connection with the parts that it covered. Looked at in this light we can perhaps see why the glove has played so great a role in popular superstition, for it covers the hand which is not only the symbol of labour but of authority. Traditionally a glove served as the gage of battle and represented love, greeting and power and thus its role in social history must have been immense. While glove superstitions as a whole have in some respects diminished to the degree that the glove has become less common as an article of dress, one in particular is so well entrenched in popular custom to be worthy of special mention. It is a common belief that to pick up one's dropped glove brings bad luck, but on the other hand should any other person do so and give it to its owner he may anticipate a pleasant surprise. This is without doubt a relic of the old gage of love motif in which the gallant who picked up his mistress's glove could expect to receive from her as his reward some very positive token of her affections.

Similar superstitions are also associated with stockings. Oddly enough the left stocking must always be put on before the right if the luck is to be maintained. So strongly entrenched is this superstition in some families that, in a recently discovered example, whenever a new pair of socks was purchased the wife of the wearer inserted a couple of stitches of different coloured cotton in each to make absolutely certain of distinguishing the one from the other. The strict observance of this rite was supposed to be a guarantee of success at the football pools.

Women's stockings have a peculiar lore of their own. If a nylon stocking slips three times from the suspender when it is being fastened it is a sure sign that the day is destined to be unlucky. In another modern superstition should nylon stockings or tights while drying on the line curl around each other in intimate embrace it is a sure sign of joy and happiness to come. A ladder or hole which occurs in both stockings simultaneously is a promise that a substantial gift will be received in the same week. Incidentally, any woman desiring to see a vision of her future husband or lover should place her suspender belt beneath her pillow and sleep on it. Formerly it would have been her garter that was used, this being a symbol of luck, and especially luck in love.

Women, particularly the younger ones, appear to have developed a philosophy of clothing which occupies a halfway position between ordinary association of ideas and superstition. In common with teenage girls they often tend to condemn as unlucky a dress that becomes associated with an unhappy experience when worn for the first time. On the other hand women do not necessarily regard a garment which has favourable associations as a luck-bringer. Some of them believe, however, that to put a garment on inside out is lucky for love. New clothing, representing a new beginning, has its own distinctive superstitions. In some places in the north east of England a boy with a new suit is taken to his relatives and presented with a new coin which is placed in his pocket. At such a time it is customary to make a wish. New clothing is worn at Easter to synchronise with the season of spring and renewal.

Clothing fetishism has apparently reached its high water mark in the era of the pop idol. In a newspaper report the misadventures of the famous Dave Clark Five pop group are described. Following a "session" at Hull, "We were smuggled out of the side door down to our own car. We were still wearing our stage suits. Then it all happened. Hundreds of fans broke through the police cordon and pounced on us. The pockets of my leather coat were torn off and the trousers ripped . . . they even tore out our hair." Articles wrenched from the living bodies of pop idols not infrequently become vested with quasi-supernatural powers, but on the other hand the fetish has been likened to ritual cannibalism, in which the body of a chieftain is eaten by his fellow tribesmen as a means of acquiring his powers.

Among the most potent of clothing superstitions is that concerning new shoes and it is also the most widespread. New shoes placed on a table will never be worn : they are intended for the long march of the dead into the underworld. This is sometimes reinterpreted as an omen of loss of one's job. Shoelace lore insists that for a shoelace to come undone at the commencement of an enterprise is most unlucky. On the other hand it is lucky to discover the shoelaces knotted. Among primitive people a knot is often regarded as an amulet that protects one from the attacks of evil spirits. Perhaps one of the strangest of surviving superstitions is the belief that the clothes of the dead should never be worn since, like their original owners, they are destined to rot away.

From an object that is worn to one that is carried is but a single step in the logic of the superstitious mind. The very name "umbrella", from the Latin umbra, shade, is a reminder that this useful article was originally a sunshade used by royalty in Africa and the ancient East. Because of its close association with the sun and because also it symbolises the solar wheel, it became a kind of sacrilege to open an umbrella in the shade, which was out of the sun's domain, and from this there developed the well-known superstition that it is unlucky to open an umbrella inside the house. The superstition as applied today, however, does not extend to umbrella shops where the fates and the righteous anger of the sun may be defied with impunity. The superstition doubtless received reinforcement from the fact that umbrellas were used by clergy-men at the burial of the dead before they were adopted by the public as a whole

Those who buy handbags should be aware that for luck a new handbag or purse should always contain a luck penny, this being a magical device to ensure a continuous supply of money in the future. In dream symbolism an empty purse is a promise of money to come; a full one an omen of penury.

It is one of our hoariest superstitions that the colour green is unlucky. There has been a good deal of speculation as to the origins of this well-known phobia which, in the writer's opinion, might well have been derived from an association of ideas connect-ing a "green churchyard" with death which is also expressed in the saying, "A green Christmas means a full churchyard". On the other hand if green was the colour supposed to have been peculiar to the fairy-race of mythology, wearing clothes of this colour would most certainly have placed the wearer within their power.

The calamitous influence of the colour green provides the stimulus for many superstitious anecdotes. In one of these, so the author was assured, it was immediately following the gift of a green blouse to an old lady that, apparently without any previous warning, she suddenly fell dead, as if conforming with the old saying, "If you wear green your relatives will soon wear black". Humanity is ever on the lookout for signs that will confirm its gravest fears. Green wallpaper still creates a degree of apprehen-sion in some quarters since it is supposed to exude arsenic which, being absorbed into the body of the sleeper, results in death. Brown, for clothing, is ill-omened because as the colour of the monkish habit it represents poverty, penitence and sorrow, as well as the earth of the graveyard.

The superstitions associated with the various colours are well worthy of further investigation in view of the close association existing between colour and the emotions. Brilliant colours are

usually adopted during youth, but with age they give way grace-
fully to cream, beige and pastel shades as if responsive to declining
vitality. The power of colour generally in the realm of superstition
has more recently received support from non-superstitious sources
and colour therapy is well established as one of the methods
employed by the medical "fringe". Traditionally, red, white and
blue are happy colours, while black, yellow, purple and orange are
notoriously bad-luck bringers. Modern researchers like nothing better than to delve deeply into colour symbolism as a factor in
market research. A survey conducted recently among London
bachelors revealed that sex was associated with red, and death for
some astounding reason with black.

Jewellery occupies an even far more vital role in the superstitious scheme of things than clothing, since almost invariably jewels
were originally employed for the purpose of keeping evil spirits at
bay. The hostile forces surrounding every individual were thought
to seek entry into the body by means of one of the five orifices and
for this reason it was necessary to set up some magical system of
defence. Earrings were originally talismanic charms to protect the
aperture of the ear, while nose rings performed a like function for
the nose. The eyes and mouth were protected for their part by
painted or tattooed designs, as were the finger and toe nails.
During the course of ages and with the decline in the more
primitive aspects of devil fear, pigmentation and ornamentation
apparently became associated with the idea of attraction rather
than repulsion, while nail-painting and similar decorations were
elevated to status symbols, being signs of superior rank. Finger
rings, however, which were originally thought to possess great
magical power are still to some considerable extent objects of
superstition, particularly the wedding ring which, as a perfect
circle, symbolises unity and eternity, hence the prevailing superstition that a broken ring is an omen of a broken relationship. A
similar association of ideas is at work behind the engagement ring
superstition communicated to the author recently. An engaged girl
showed her ring to a friend who immediately placed it on the third
finger of her left hand and twisted it three times for luck while
counting ten, which was apparently a device intended to guarantee
favourable prospects for her own engagement.

Ornamental jewellery, because of its close association with the
emotions, will often acquire a reputation for good or bad luck
purely as the result of association of ideas. Like the dress with

unhappy associations, an object of jewellery which becomes connected in the mind of its wearer with some misadventure becomes in effect a jinx. The jewel with the most notorious record for bringing disaster is the emerald, yet it would appear that this stone acquired its ill-omened reputation only in comparatively modern times largely as the result of the many travellers' tales current at the close of the last century, the theme of which was the curse that beset explorers who had the temerity to steal the emerald eyes of sacred Buddhas from oriental temples. Likewise the opal, which despite its reputation of being "good for the eyes", became an unlucky stone as the direct result of its sinister role in Sir Walter Scott's novel *Anne of Geierstein*, a character who disappeared after holy water fell on the opal in her hair.

The Hope Diamond, as it became known, is another notorious ill-luck bringer which brought disaster to whosoever had the misfortune to come into possession of it, the original thief dying in torment in the jaws of wild beasts. Marie Antoinette's necklace, when put up for auction in India in 1968, found no buyer since whoever owns it is doomed to die leaving no heir.

It is one of the most common of our jewellery superstitions that a gift of pearls brings tears, yet closer study will reveal the thinking process which gave rise to this misconception. In medieval times, because of its appearance, the pearl was known as a "solidified dewdrop" and this can clearly be seen as but a short step from its modern definition as a "solidified tear drop" with its overtones of sorrow. Oddly enough, sorrow does not fall upon those who receive pearls in the form of an heirloom. It is only in the form of a gift that its evil magic can operate. The ancient doctrine that precious stones possess inherent magical qualities that somehow influences not only the fortunes but the emotional state of the wearer, is responsible for the curious and useful superstition that an amethyst, an amulet against nervous diseases, can cure intoxication. In fact, in the past, wine was actually drunk from amethyst cups to protect the drinker from the consequences of over-imbibing. Tension and anxiety can also be banished if one wears a sapphire. According to an old poem:

> A woman born when Autumn leaves
> Are rustling in the September breeze
> A sapphire on her brow should bind.
> 'Twil cure diseases of the mind.

It also brings luck in love and if of a pale colour will cure impotence.

Diamonds, it would appear, are still regarded as great luck-bringers, particularly to those born under the sign of Aries the Ram, and it is a common belief that "to receive a piece of jewellery containing diamonds brings a change of fortune". Modern jewellers have capitalised upon the astounding revival of astrology in the twentieth century by their patronage of birthstone superstitions of which there are a number of different systems.

Amber :	health
Amethyst :	peace and repose
Aquamarine :	aids optimism
Carbuncle :	reassures when in danger
Coral :	aids friendship
Chrysolite :	protects against gout and madness
Diamond :	drives away insanity
Emerald :	fertility, hope and immortality
Garnet :	physical strength
Jade :	mental power
Lapis Lazuli :	dispels melancholia
Onyx :	clarity of sight and mind
Opal :	confidence
Pearl :	beauty
Ruby :	charity and dignity
Sapphire :	innocence
Topaz :	integrity
Turquoise :	success

Magic stones and jewellery without doubt provide a strongpoint of modern superstitious beliefs among individuals who would repudiate with scorn any suggestion of witchcraft, whether of the black or white variety.

Finally then to the most potent and pervading of superstitious practice, practically a form of black magic on its own, employed for the express purpose of fascinating and ensnaring the male. The art of the perfumer is closely associated with magic, the very word fascination being originally associated with the power of the evil eye over its helpless victim. There even exists a quite unfounded belief that the eighteenth-century House of Commons seriously considered instituting a law to the effect that "all women who imposed upon any of His Majesty's subjects by the use of scents" should be punished as witches. As long ago as the 1930s collectors of superstitious revivals were drawing attention to the same underlying theme in the choice of psychic names for perfumes in the United States, some examples being "Tabu", "Love Potion", "Witchery" and "Spellbound".

Even the sweetmeats intended for the fascination of the loved one have become involved in the arcana of superstition, as all consumers of exotically named brands of chocolates must know. What chocolate connoisseurs are probably unaware of is that chocolate or chocolatl was originally a magical aphrodisiac and that in old Europe those who sold cups of chocolate were denounced by the purists for inflaming the lusts of the flesh.

CHAPTER VII

COUNTRY MAGIC

IT IS one of the more powerful misconceptions among townsmen—almost a superstition in fact—that rural life today provides a framework favourable to the survival of occult beliefs belonging to an earlier culture. It is supposed also that because of the inter-relationship between the agricultural year and the procession of the seasons, the farmworker is conscious of a closer affinity to the life of the spirit than his urbanised neighbour. Alas, this is no more than a metropolitan dream. Now, as in the immediate past, the farm-labourer's environment provides little scope for romanticism. Until not so long ago it consisted exclusively of a regime of overwork, underpayment, bad housing, squalor and ingrained ignorance, not to mention a lifelong fear of sickness and of course of the workhouse where the labourer was so often condemned to end his days.

It was in fact because of this poverty, ignorance and separation from the mainstream of communication that the old-time country-man remained dependent for so many of his ideas upon oral traditions that had been abandoned by the townsman generations earlier. Only an artist or a poet can go into raptures about winter in the countryside : to the farmworker the open air can be hell.

The great change in outlook for the countryman began with the introduction of popular education a century ago. From that time onwards, as the older generation died out one by one, the oral lore of the past was growingly displaced by "book learning" of a far from folksy character. Folklore in fact means little to the country-man, associated as it is with the era of hunger and leaking roofs. It is the townsman, and more often the schoolteacher, who has brought *olde tyme* customs back to the countryside, reviving what were often almost extinct and certainly quite obsolete beliefs.

Now, in the second half of the twentieth century, the social revolution has at long last reached the life of the countryside. The farmworker is slightly better paid and better housed than before, but he remains a practical man and old customs, whether superstitious or otherwise, have been readily surrendered for the more powerful magic of a living wage, while his sense of the miraculous is today largely confined to a touching faith in winning football pools.

The remoteness of rural life has retreated before the advance of the automobile, and the telephone and television have completed the process. In Great Britain, perhaps the most highly mechanised agricultural economy in the world, the revolution is almost complete. In Ireland and parts of Wales and Scotland, however, there remain isolated pockets of the older traditions, and even in England in quite unexpected places there may occasionally be found fragments of the old country lore, relics of what was once a comprehensive rural philosophy.

As one might expect, where the superstitions of rural life have survived they are largely confined to the children. It may be impossible today to discover any individual within twenty miles of London who seriously believes that stones grew as plants do, but such a belief can still occasionally be found among children in remote parts of East Anglia; it is perhaps a last fragment of the ancient philosophy that regarded every object of creation as obeying the same immutable laws : that logically if plants and trees grew, then so must stones. This subject is developed more fully by Christina Hole, Editor of the *Encyclopedia of Superstition*, where she says : "The idea that small stones often found in fields have grown there and that consequently it is useless to attempt to clear the ground by picking them off was once very common." She observes that the belief was general in Suffolk up to some ninety years ago.

If any of the older countrymen can be persuaded to talk about old-time rural superstitions, and the opportunity usually occurs only after a fairly lengthy acquaintance, some amazing revelations will sometimes be brought to the light of day. One is usually assured, however, that lore of this kind belongs to the dead past and is now extinct. The older superstitions, even if they are no longer accepted, are always worth noting, however, if only because they are the ancestors of the ones we hold today.

Rural superstitions up to the end of the last century were nicely balanced affairs, every psychic ill-wind that blew being offset by some protective device which was a precious relic of handed-down magical lore. On the one hand there was the witch, a common myth at that time, who was held responsible for what we would now call bad luck; and on the other the village wise-man or woman who saw to it that the knavish tricks of the witch were properly frustrated.

ASTROLOGASTER,
OR,
THE FIGVRE-CASTER.

Rather the Arraignment of Artlesse Astrologers, and Fortune-tellers
that cheat many ignorant people vnder the pretence of foretelling things to
come, of telling things that are past, finding out things that are lost &x.
pounding Dreames, calculating Deaths and Natiuities,
once againe brought to the Barre.

By Iohn Melton.

Cicero. *Stultorum plena sunt omnia.*

Imprinted at London by *Barnard Alsop*, for *Edward Blackmore*, and are
to be sold in *Paules* Churchyard, at the Signe of the
Blazing-Starre. 1620. ƒ

There are more things in heaven and earth than in your philosophy.

Guardian of the threshold—a Pharaoh's head.

BICKERSTAFF's
ALMANACK:

OR, A

Vindication of the STARS,

From all the False Imputations, and Erroneous Assertions, of the late *JOHN PARTRIDGE*, and all other Mistaken Astrologers whatever.

AS ALSO,

A Brief Account of what Things are Truly Occasioned by the Influence of *Celestial Bodies*: Proving, That the Art of Telling Fortunes, is an Imposture upon Innocent Persons by *Mock-Astrologers* and *Gypsies*.

For the YEAR 1710.

Nullum Numen abeft, si sit Prudentia ; sed Te Nos facimus, Fortuna, Deam, Cæloq; locamus ! Ju.

While all each other with kind Wishes chear, And Neighbour-Salutations joy the Year, Live free (ye *Britons*) from Domestick Strife : Ask Heav'n all else in one ; ask *ANNA*'s Life.

By *ISAAC BICKERSTAFF Esq;* Student in Astrology, Commentator on the Occult Sciences, and One of the Eighth Order of Poets of the Cities of London and Westminster.

LONDON:
Printed for the Company of STATIONERS, *Anno Æræ Christiana* 1710.

Under the pseudonym of Isaac Bickerstaff, Jonathan Swift ridiculed John Partridge's Prophetic Almanack.

Today witchcraft and its representatives have moved to the towns, and the countryman is left with little more than a vague memory that such people once existed. Up to sixty years ago, relics of the old witchcraft beliefs were still fairly strong in East Anglia; sick cows that were thought to be under a spell had their tails cut until they bled by way of remedy.

In the Dengie Hundred of Essex one comes across stories about individuals who in any other age would have been called witches. Some countrymen, it would appear—and not so long ago at that—were supposed to possess a secret power to hold up all the labour of a farm by bewitching the tools. In the words of one old Latchingdon labourer: "They'd stop you working . . . couldn't move your tools. You'd stick your fork into the ground and couldn't get it out again. So you'd have to 'hustle' it . . . thrash the fork with a stick before you could pull it out of the ground."

In rural East Anglia the modern concept of the jinxed machine took a more positive shape in the past than it does in today's modern factory. Anecdotes were told illustrating the power of the evil eye to cause a breakdown in steam threshing machines, and how farmers were coerced into awarding increases of wages by the baleful glance of some farmworker who had the hallmark of the witch—eyebrows that met across the top of the nose.

Even today one occasionally hears suggestions of "witchcraft" in the countryside, usually taking the form of anecdotes about the eccentricities of some neighbour. A few years ago the author met an old countrywoman who told him something of her philosophy of magical lore, which was largely restricted to the superstitions of fear and death. It is still of interest, if only because it indicates the intensity of the power of evil that must have existed until comparatively recently in darkest England:

"When you first hold a new baby it should wet in the fireplace. It will then be clean and well-behaved.

"Never dress a baby in black if you wish it to live. If you change its winter clothing before May it will die.

"Before it reaches the age of five a young child is under the protection of a familiar spirit.

"Silent pools in forest glades are evil, but still pools are unlucky and to see your reflection in them dangerous.

"A weir is unlucky—never stand at 'the meeting place' of the waters.

"When you hear your name called by an inner voice that person is thinking of you.

"If you think you recognise someone who approaches you and find yourself mistaken it is an omen of that person's forthcoming death.

"If there is a 'presence' in the room the candle will diminish and go out.

"If you wish someone to die, begrudge them everything they have. Everything will wither and die—and they also.

"The will-o'-the-wisp is a phantom light that entices people to their deaths."

This is without doubt the creed of fear which has prevailed from medieval times until almost yesterday, but it clearly indicates that what we tend now to write off as "superstitions" must have been of supreme significance in the relationship of the individual to the environment in the older closed societies.

Trading on superstition does not have quite the same pernicious role today as in the past when the witch-fearing farmer was often persuaded to part with considerable sums of money for the protection of his stock against bad luck. Such "protection money" was one of the permanent tolls levied on the nineteenth-century superstitious farmer by certain unscrupulous blackmailers called Cunning Men, who were finally driven out of business when a better-educated rural population began to discard its beliefs in magic. Yet superstition, if ejected by one door, can be guaranteed to re-enter by another. Luck money, which is a token payment demanded at the time of a sale of livestock to ensure good fortune for the transaction, can still lead to exploitation. An article appeared in *The Times* recently complaining of the menace of luck money at auctions. It declared : "The price of drink for good luck with the animals is one thing but the custom of paying a pound or even two is an imposition." It goes on to say : "Vendors not paying their £1 or £2 rightly or wrongly fear for the future sales of their livestock either in price or difficulties that might arise after the sale." A dealer who exploits luck money, it appears, can make large sums tax free.

A sublimated fear of the evil eye and of tempting Providence lies at the root of the almost universal belief among farmers, as among other superstitious classes, that when entering an animal for a show under no circumstances should any form of admiration or expectation of success be mentioned as this results in failure. Should such an expression be inadvertently made the owner must immediately give voice to the worst possible calamity he can imagine at this time by saying, "break your neck". On the other hand the custom of plaiting the horse's tail or mane before a competition is now maintained only as a point of style rather than as a luck-bringing device. It is said to have originated in the custom of plaiting ribbons into the animal's tail to ward off witchcraft.

Some horse breeders believe it lucky to possess an animal having on its neck a groove into which the human thumb will fit, since this is the sign of the "Prophet's thumb-print", clear evidence to the really superstitious owner that the animal is lineally descended from one of the five brood mares of the prophet Mahomet. The horse, an animal which in ancient mythology pulled the chariots of the gods, is still associated with many curious superstitious beliefs. The breath of a piebald pony, for example, is supposed to be a cure for whooping cough. In Devonshire a horse with four white feet brings misfortune, though the approach of a horse with "white stockings" promises a happy change in one's fortunes.

It is far from generally known that the belief still exists in many rural areas that power can be exercised over a horse by means of a secret word, known as "The Horseman's Word". During the course of an investigation into the present-day superstitions of Norfolk, the author was astounded to discover that the existence of this magical faculty was generally accepted. The "word" itself is apparently a closely guarded secret, known only to the older generation of horsekeepers—a fast-diminishing company—and is regarded with superstitious awe.

Children, especially schoolgirls, are great horse-lovers and this provides one of the possible explanations for the survival of so many superstitions about horses in the automobile age. Among modern-minded adults, however, the horse has almost entirely lost its aura as an object of magic and mythology, and the vogue for horse-brasses as decor in public houses is quite unconnected with their original role as amulets for protecting so valuable an animal against the evil eye. The superstition-monger may find it profitable, however, to look more closely at the designs of the brasses, since these bear all the signs of having originated in ancient magical doctrines, the crescent being the symbol of moon worship, while the heart and sun motifs came down to us from that most superstitious of civilisations, ancient Egypt.

The traditional countryman's lucky charm, the holed stone or hagstone, which so often in the past was hung on the stable door as an amulet against misfortune to the farm stock, has never quite lost its influence among countryfolk, and whenever one is found it is always carefully preserved as a novelty, and sometimes for good luck. Such charms come to light not infrequently in the older barns and there is always a superstitious objection by the owners to their removal.

Among the older rural superstitions which have managed to survive the impact of modern change relatively intact, is the belief that it is lucky if the first lamb seen in the spring has its head turned in the direction of the onlooker, while in Wales the first appearance of a black sheep among the flock is often greeted with the words, "First luck black sheep". This attitude reflects the almost universal conviction that the first appearance of any new thing, whether animal or plant, is a token of good fortune representing a kind of "beginner's luck". Arising from this superstition, country children will make a wish when eating the first new potato of the year. The first of any series, whether it is the first-born among human beings or the first day of the New Year, has always been of occult significance.

Before leaving the superstitions of animal life one should perhaps mention the widely held belief that the pig has the power to "see the wind". This is undoubtedly a relic of the old worship of the Teutonic Sun Boar which was supposed to have command over the winds of the heavens.

Birds, once regarded as winged messengers of the gods, still remain a focal point for many rural superstitions. The presence of dark-plumaged birds—notably the crow—should one perch on a roof, is ill-omened and suggestive of death. The bad name of the crow, however, was originally inherited from the raven, which as the symbol of doom was displayed on the banners of the wild Norse invaders of these lands. In Iceland, which was originally settled by the Norsemen, it is believed that if a raven flies in your direction it is an omen of death.

The owl has long been a bird of fear and is even today associated in the popular mind with the forces of darkness. In terms of superstition it is unlucky when an owl flies low. No ghost story is worth the telling without its background of melancholy hooting from among the threatening trees, and it is generally accepted that the constant cries of an owl constitute a death omen. Oddly enough the white owl is sacred in India because of its colour. In the west the owl's reputation as a bird of wisdom springs equally from folklore and mythology, for this bird was associated in ancient Greece with the goddess of wisdom, Pallas Athene, and was adopted as its symbol by the city of Athens.

Bats occupy a halfway position between the terrestrial and aerial creatures of the night and are therefore deeply involved in superstitions. Should bats fly low and touch a human being with their wings it is an unlucky omen, perhaps of death. There exists a strongly-held but quite unfounded idea that bats have a predilection for becoming trapped in a woman's hair.

The magpie, an oracular bird, seems to have exerted a peculiar fascination over mankind, from earliest times doubtless because of the rarity of black and white in Nature's colour scheme. As a messenger from the gods it conveys good news (white) and evil portents (black). In the west of England it is saluted on sight and Scottish children mark the significance of meeting it with the rhyme :

> One means anger, two brings mirth.
> Three a wedding, four a birth.
> Five is heaven—Six is hell.
> But seven's the very De'il's ain sell.

Among luck-bringing birds are the robin and the swallow. The sight of the first robin of the year must always be followed by making a wish. The robin, because of its red breast, was long associated by our pagan ancestors with the gods of fire, and was believed to be a bird of great magical power. Despite being among the best loved of birds it is sometimes feared when it enters a house or a church, for its presence there is an omen of death. The swallow is generally regarded as a messenger of hope and the destruction of its nest, therefore, brings a certainty of disaster to the offender.

Among the best known agents of latter-day rustic divination is the cuckoo whose voice, if first heard coming from the right, betokens a lucky year, but if from the left an unlucky one.

Country superstitions belong to the childhood of the race and, perhaps appropriately, are now largely confined to children, being of far less moment to the matter-of-fact rural adult for whom the world of Nature has ceased to symbolise cosmic unity and which has lost also its religious significance. Not so long ago in the English countryside the snake was supposed to have an inherent power to heal the sick. Even so it is surprising that a snakeskin should still occasionally be utilised as an inside band for hats in cases of persistent headache. Quite extinct today, however, is the analogous custom of using an eelskin garter for cramp. Snakes, like eels, are supposed, quite erroneously, not to be able to die before the sun has set. The snake has acquired its important role in superstition as a direct product of its power to cast its skin, and for this reason it has always been regarded as a symbol of immortality.

Among our insects the bee is one of the few invested with an aura of sanctity. This is of great interest because bees were anciently regarded as messengers of the gods, and it is noticeable how even today when they enter a house great care is undertaken to liberate them without injury. In Wales a bee flying round a sleeping child is a promise of a life of happiness. The custom of "Telling the Bees" of a death in the family is not entirely extinct today, although the elaborate ritual of tying a piece of black crepe to the hive has been abandoned, perhaps for ever. The quiet words uttered to the hive : "Bees, bees, your master's dead" are probably all that survives of one of the most ancient of superstitions. It is a subject that is rarely discussed by bee-keepers, perhaps from fear of ridicule, or alternately from a sense of reverence.

The association of the spider with money is complicated on the one hand by the fact that as a Christian symbol it is the bleeder of the poor, and because of its other role as a symbol of industry. When discovered in clothing the spider means money to come. In rural Suffolk the "money spider", known as the "money spinner", is picked up in the hand and whirled three times round the head as a device to bring wealth. Among Nature's signs of death to the countryman who has ears to hear are the ticking spider, the chirping cricket and the whistling mouse. Unexplained knocking is supposed to foretell a death, so the tapping sound of the death-watch beetle within a house is similarly feared—this notion is by no means confined to the country.

Beetles, of the black variety, are closely linked with weather magic, and many children believe that killing a black beetle brings rain. Blackness in sympathetic magic is suggestive of rain-clouds. Luckier is the ladybird, a traditional favourite which, because of its red colour, was once associated with the ancient gods of fire. This explains the well-known children's chant :

> Ladybird, ladybird, fly away home
> Your house is on fire and your children are gone."

Like the bee, the ladybird often receives the help of humanity when in distress. Behind this type of reverence one detects a respect for the old magical qualities with which so many creatures of the wild were once credited.

Trees were once regarded as the abodes of spirits and as late as the tenth century had their secret worshippers. The reverence for trees is still very much alive however and is partly responsible for many of our superstitions. This respect is most obvious when some stately avenue becomes threatened by the axe for then one can always anticipate an outcry. The rowan and the thorn remain sacred trees because their harvests of berries represent the provision made by the gods for feeding the birds in winter. Out of this pleasing tradition has grown the belief that a heavy crop of berries is an omen of a hard winter, this once again being an expression of the old doctrine that coming events cast their shadow before and a touching faith in the providence of nature.

The folk memory that trees are in some mysterious way linked with the life of man is a very ancient one. Among the Teutons the destruction of a tree could be a crime punishable by death, for every tree had its own peculiar occult properties. In northern Europe it was once held that the life and success of the householder and his family were bound up with the fate of the tree that was ceremoniously planted when the foundations of the house were laid. A relic of this curious belief is the European custom of "topping-out"— attaching a fir tree to the roof of the house. In Ireland one still finds symbols of old-time tree worship in the presence of a fairy tree, either a blackthorn or a white thorn, growing at the very centre of a cultivated field, a site still sacrosanct against the invasion of the plough, and in deference to the sacred tree roads have actually been re-routed. Similarly, a single holly may sometimes be seen standing amid the growing corn of Suffolk fields, sacrosanct because it is considered a "holy" tree. The superstitious Irish were, in pre-Christian times, dedicated arboreal worshippers, each tribe possessing its own sacred tree. The blackthorn has ominous properties in the British Isles, and in the Welsh border country bringing its blossoming branch into the house means a death in the family. In Scotland the rowan or mountain ash is the traditional protector of the household against witchcraft and is still planted as a luck-bringer. The weeping willow, the emblem of grief, continues to manifest its traditionally mournful associations, one very remarkable example being the discovery in 1964 at Rochford, Essex, of a willow branch, together with other deathly symbols, buried in a carefully dug grave on the golf course by some modern sorcerer.

The oak was the ancient ceremonial tree of the Druids, and its "golden bough", the mistletoe, was sacred to Thor, god of thunder. From this arises the very common superstition that an oak tree is never struck by lightning and likewise the well-known belief that cutting an oak brings bad luck. Sometimes in the countryside one sees a carved oak set in stone above a gateway to protect the house against the lightning.

The elder is said to have been the tree upon which Judas hanged himself, and in pagan times it was used for human sacrifice. There still exists a country superstition that those who burn elderwood bring death into the home. In Cornwall one occasionally discovers individuals who will always bow to an elder before cutting it down.

A further relic of this old-style deference to the once sacred giants of the forest is the still surviving custom of placing coins under trees that have been planted to commemorate some important event. The basic intention behind this ceremony is that money is a source of power and that its sacrifice must therefore promote growth. In Scotland this type of "sacrifice" is known as a "luck penny".

Foresters sometimes observe ancient tree rites with little knowledge of their mystical origins. In Epping Forest in Essex, for example, when the chairman of the Conservationists retires, a ceremonial tree is planted and a plaque attached. (Incidentally, there is a superstition that the appearance of a white doe in Epping Forest always presages some calamity.)

Sometimes the birth of a child, or an important event like a coronation, is commemorated by the ritual planting of a tree, a modern form of the ancient belief that the welfare of the community is indissolubly bound up with the life of its trees.

Among fruit-bearing trees the apple is generally regarded as unlucky, and the pear lucky. The ill-repute of the apple may be due to an old custom in certain lands of placing an apple in the hand of a dead child, quite independently of the sombre associations of this fruit with the Fall of Eve and the tragic ejection from Paradise. A ceremony known as Wassailing the Apple Tree still takes place in the west of England to ensure a plentiful crop of fruit; it entails baptising the branches in cider and firing guns to drive away evil spirits.

The blackberry is the source of a curious superstition which is surprisingly strong all over the British Isles, and even as far away as the Orkneys, to the effect that it is unlucky to gather this fruit after October 11th, Old Michaelmas Day. This arises from the medieval tradition that it was on this particular day that Satan was thrown out of Heaven and that as he landed on earth his foot touched a blackberry bush, which he trampled and spat upon in his rage; hence the belief that blackberries eaten after this date cause sickness and even death. This can clearly be seen as a rationalisation, a mystical inference derived from the fact that blackberries at about this time of the year begin to reach the woody over-ripe stage when they start to become inedible.

Perhaps only very young children are likely today to retain any appreciation of the inherent magic of wild flowers. In ancient times flowers were an essential ingredient of harvest and seasonal festivals and perhaps naturally became involved with the supernaturalism with which mankind invested the wonders he saw around him in the world. In the country they still say that if the broom is heavy with blossom the crops may also be expected to be heavy; they also add that when the broom is out of season kissing is out of favour for this is a plant to be found flowering the whole year round! Clover, which is said to have been used by the Druids to charm away evil spirits, is especially lucky if four-leaved, yet even seven-leaved clovers are now in cultivation by an enterprising Yorkshire firm. There is a comparatively modern superstition—a relic of wartime—which holds that if you wear a four-leaved clover as a buttonhole you may hope to evade military service.

Heather is always lucky, the white variety particularly so, since white was once a sacred colour. One explanation for this superstition is that only the white heather is free of the bloodstains of the Picts who were so cruelly slaughtered by their enemies. That heather has a traditional connection with bloodshed is echoed in the superstition at Culloden that "heather will never grow over the graves of the clans".

The may, the flower of the hawthorn, was once a luck-bringer, and prior to the calendar change of 1752 was always brought home by young people to deck the houses on May morning. Now that it blooms eleven days later it has assumed, for some unknown reason, the character of a death plant, and to bring it into the house brings sorrow. In one version of the superstition the wearing of may in the buttonhole or carrying it indoors means a death in the family within the year.

Ancient man apparently regarded all unexpected change in nature as extremely ominous and for this reason the unseasonable blooming of flowers or ripening of fruit were seen to represent a dangerous departure from the normal course of events and clear signs of some forthcoming disaster. The first appearance of an ill-omened symbol was even more fearful to his mind. The first snowdrop of the season is still not brought into the house for this reason, for its petals, with their resemblance to a shroud, are emblems of death and can cast their sinister blight upon the family.

The old tradition that a corn dolly plaited from the last sheaves taken from the harvest field is the spirit of the corn has received an unexpected boost in recent times, for now dollys, manufactured by folksy-minded members of Women's Institutes, are in growing demand as luck-bringers.

Much of the superstitious lore of the countryside was originally concerned with the weather. The dictum "red sky at night, shepherds' delight" is probably as sound today as in the past, when accurate forecasting was absolutely essential to the domestic economy. Less scientifically justifiable perhaps is the superstition that a red sky on New Year's Day presages political disorders and grave distress in the twelve months ahead. The collection of scientific weather statistics is a science little more than a century old, and the age-old wisdom based on first-hand observation is probably just as effective in the long run, despite the fact that most of it has been written off as superstition. A friend who was informed by a shepherd on the Isle of Wight that a holiday taken on that island in the first ten days of October could be assured of good weather took the trouble to check the information over a period of ten years, and found the prediction strikingly accurate.

Right down to the present time, certain rain-making superstitions have remained relatively intact despite advances in knowledge, and re-emerge with each passing generation in an up-dated form. In primitive communities a pot of water would be poured upon the parched earth in times of drought as a libation to the rain gods, who would then be expected to imitate the action with a shower of rain, and in some parts of modern Wales children are "chidden" when they spill water, in case this brings on a rainstorm. Gardeners everywhere remain firm believers in the old wives' tale that if they hose their lawns rain will surely follow as if in mockery of their efforts. The ancient custom among savages of firing arrows into the air in the hope of bursting the clouds and making rain, is paralleled by the belief sometimes held in coastal districts of Britain that gunfire can cause a downpour. The old superstition that Queen Victoria's public ceremonies were always blessed with fine weather originated from the supposed power of a salute of twenty-one guns (representing the multiple of lucky three and lucky seven) to charm away all storms. So strongly entrenched was the myth that the South African authorities attempted in 1895 to break a drought by firing guns into the sky, this action being condemned by the whole Boer population as a direct defiance of God. A modern development of the same theme lies behind the superstition that the atom bomb and the rocket are responsible for outbreaks of bad weather. This belief became very fashionable in the United States of America during the immediate post-war years.

Space travel is now blamed for the same crime against nature and in the latest manifestation of this superstition the campaign to rid the air of pollution is held responsible for the disturbance of atmospheric conditions.

In our never-ending search for mystical explanations for natural phenomena, we go on repeating the same old myths just so long as they can be disguised in a conventional garb. Many of the older weather superstitions live on in the countryside where opening an umbrella inside a house is supposed to bring both misfortune and rain. In East Anglia it is sometimes considered unlucky to cut down trees, since this increases rain "by altering the basis of the weather". The mystical figure three crops up in the superstition that three frosts will be followed by rain, or alternatively that three frosts will be automatically succeeded by a black frost.

Storms can create such havoc in the female mind that one might well imagine faith in Thor the thunder god to be a living religion, for women continue to seek refuge under tables and cover the mirrors in order to prevent what is described as the "deflection" of lightning on to the occupants of the house. Doors and windows are often opened during thunderstorms to facilitate the passage of the thunder blast through the building without damage to the structure. Our whole "philosophy" of thunder superstitions seems to be based upon the assumption that the sky gods are selective in the objects they attack— hence the completely unfounded superstition that lightning never strikes twice in the same place. The ominous implications of un-seasonable natural phenomena are responsible for the superstition that thunder in winter portends disaster in the forthcoming summer.

The minor eddies of wind which sometimes swirl around a farm-yard were once believed to be whirling demons. Today, near Maid-stone, Kent, I found that the character of the superstition has changed and farmers regard the eddy as a good-luck sign.

Despite the fact that the moon has at last capitulated to the astronaut lunar superstitions continue to maintain a fairly strong hold over most of us. Many people are unwilling to sleep exposed to the rays of a full moon, not so much from fear of lunacy as from an irrational terror of its pale light. Some women even believe that pregnancy follows sleeping in moonlight. On the other hand the moon is often regarded as a helpful agent in agricultural matters. Also, the weather is said to alter with the new moon. However, it is purely from a superstitious tradition that we turn over a silver coin at the first sight of the new moon, for the coin is a symbolic moon which we hope will grow in numbers as the moon waxes in size. The wish we utter at the same time is a modernised form of the prayer once addressed to the moon goddess.

The supposed influence of the moon over human affairs was at one time quite remarkable. Until well into the last century many farmers only embarked upon new ventures or took fresh journeys with a waxing moon, since to have done otherwise would have linked their fortunes to a declining phase, which represented to their minds a certainty of failure.

The new moon is a harbinger of good fortune; it is unlucky, therefore, to look at it through glass, or through the branches of a tree, since these form barriers between the looker and his luck.

Even the stars in their courses, despite all the claims of the astronomers, refuse to capitulate to the scientific scheme of things and for some people a star is still equated with a human life. Many a mother, looking up into the mysterious heavens and seeing a falling star, will tell her child that somewhere someone has at that moment died, and so help to keep alive the age-old myth that the heavens watch over human destinies.

The privilege of seeing the stars is now reserved in the main to countryfolk or to those at sea. The intensive lighting and smoky effluent of towns and cities denies to their inhabitants the glories of the sky at night, and for this reason the older stellar superstitions tend more and more to fall into disuse. In their place rules the pseudo-science of astrology, the sophisticated ghost of the older folklore of the heavens.

Rural ghosts are perhaps not so plentiful today as in the past when every crossroads was haunted by the suicide, buried in that place with a stake through his or her heart, nor are there as many phantom coaches, or headless white ladies hovering near bridges and castle ruins. There once was in the country a complete estab-

Sigils and pentacles—from a 19th-century English book of prophecy.

Charles I had a forewarning that he would lose his head when the knob of his staff fell to the ground.

The Puritans, inveterate enemies of superstition, condemned Christmas as a pagan rite.

lishment of spectres that continued their hauntings for centuries on end, quite undisturbed by time and unthreatened by the site-developer. Now they display a growing tendency to vanish without trace, particularly the phantom calves and horses which once roamed the fields at night.

However, the modern countryman, even if he has discarded most of the older superstitious usages and omens, clings somewhat tenaciously to his belief in ghosts, although these are today far more likely to be associated with his domestic pet rather than with his farm stock. The hard-headed farmer who rejects with amusement tinged with incredulity the old wives' tale that the lowing of a cow after midnight is an omen of death is, oddly enough, quite ready to believe that his dog or cat possesses second sight, and while he outrightly rejects the Devil he is perfectly prepared to concede the existence of the poltergeist.

It is quite surprising how up-dated psychic lore continues to retain its hold in the modern countryside, for many a sophisticated farmer will accept, even more readily than the townsman, the principles of extra-sensory perception, or the existence of flying saucers. These are, of course, by no means rural superstitions, but belong to the general pattern of contemporary psychic culture with its somewhat astounding open-mindedness towards every manifestation of the incredible, provided that it is presented behind a pseudo-scientific façade.

CHAPTER VIII

PAGEANTRY AND PEOPLE

SOCIAL GROUPS, like individuals, tend to maintain collective rites and rules of conduct largely because of their supposed usefulness in preserving the interests of the organisation itself. Many of these rules are in fact little more than superstitious survivals which derive their strength from the inherent hostility of the community to all forms of change. This hostility arises in the first instance from the traditional fear of new things, or from the belief that social dangers can result from too drastic a repudiation of the past.

With this in mind one can perhaps comprehend better the psychological role of national institutions and their symbols, and in particular the national flag. The latter remains, even today, the most important token of national unity, being originally a symbol of the devotion of a subject to the god to whom collective sacrifice was offered.

The concept of sacrifice is integral in national life. We see it exhorted in time of national crisis, and at the aftermath in the tribute paid to the Unknown Warrior, the belated respect offered by one section of the community to the heroic warrior caste.

At the head of the older type of national state is the monarch, whose enthronement is associated with ceremonies based upon the most primitive of magical beliefs. The anointing of the Monarch is essentially a mystical act which endows him with semi-divine powers. Little more than two hundred years ago our Kings and Queens exercised this power medically by the laying on of hands to cure the King's Evil (the old name for scrofula). The crown, the symbol of power, is based upon the nimbus of the ancient Sun God, while the sceptre is one of the last surviving examples of the magician's wand. Even the British Coronation stone—the Stone of Scone—is said to be of divine origin and, like other stones in ancient mythology, embodies supernatural powers that are intended to safeguard both King and Kingdom from evil.

With this in mind it is understandable that the monarchy

should have become the focal point of a number of collective superstitions which come to the surface at times of national crises.

The passing away of a King is heralded by violent outbursts from Nature, usually taking the form of the "Royal storm" that is said to break out at such a time. A similar outbreak is supposed to take place at the death of some less illustrious but none the less important figure of authority, one example being Lord Kitchener. Perhaps the mightiest storm of all time raged at the death of Oliver Cromwell; however in this case his enemies were only too ready to point out that great storms could be associated equally with the passing of someone who had sold his soul to the Devil.

All Nature at such times engages in the general conspiracy to provide mankind with some forewarning of the forthcoming calamity. If a crop of ash keys (the winged seed of the ash tree) should happen to fail it is seen as a sign that royalty will die within a twelvemonth. Equally, should one of the ravens in the Tower of London fly away, the Crown is doomed to fall. Perhaps this is why the Tower authorities are careful to clip the wings of these rare birds. A very similar myth obtains in Gibraltar, where it is said that only while the Barbary apes remain on the Rock will British rule continue. In the island of St. Helena a Galapagos tortoise is specially imported for the psychic defence of this British possession.

The modern decline in religious observance has resulted in the extinction of most of the superstitions of churchgoers, and these are now at a very low ebb. Here and there one discovers, however, some parishioner who believes that frequent attendance at Holy Communion can be good for his rheumatism, while the Church Bible is still occasionally resorted to for divinatory purposes, being opened at random and a pin thrust into the page, the text thus marked off being supposed to serve as a guide to the future. Whether from reverence or otherwise, there exists a strong hesitation to dispose of a Bible other than as a gift, and to burn one is even now regarded not merely as blasphemous but very unlucky.

One religious custom which certainly overlaps into the area of superstitious belief is the exorcism of poltergeists by ordained clergymen; this is one of the last surviving relics of superstitious pre-Reformation rites.

Coming events cast their shadows before in any national catastrophe and all down the corridors of time signs and portents have been looked for and discovered in any unexpected activity in Nature. Should more lambs be born than is usual, or ants become prolific, it is taken as a warning by the countryman of some holocaust to come. When more boys are born than girls it is a sure sign that Providence is preparing to replace with new stock the young men doomed to die. For the same reason it is generally accepted that more boys than girls are born in time of war. To dream of blood or to see a red moon is to receive an omen of bloody days to come. A stream in Kent known as "The Waters of Woe" is said to flow only before some war or national disaster or forthcoming conflict. In the United States the ghost of Abraham Lincoln may be expected to materialise in the White House but only, it is emphasised, on the eve of some national disaster. In England Drake's Drum begins spontaneously to beat and the folk hero King Arthur stirs in his grave.

The "screaming" skull of Bettiscombe Manor in Dorset is said to fulfil a somewhat similar role. This ghostly token from prehistoric times, which is kept on view in the manor, is closely linked in the popular mind with the fate of the nation. It is supposed to have sweated blood shortly before the First World War was declared.

Warfare seems to summon from the very depths of the psyche a power that arms the personality with the ability to overcome fear and therefore to this extent increases the chances of survival. Whole populations, from their leaders downwards, become involved in mystical rites, and the more extreme among them often make no real attempt to conceal their superstitious attitudes. Hitler took guidance from an astrologer, with the result that the British found it necessary to employ an astrologer of their own to discover what advice the Fuehrer was receiving. There is apparently no truth in the story that both astrologers were double agents. Ritual magic attains its highest peak in the collective and personal ceremonies performed by the community that is poised upon the brink of death.

In no theatre of human affairs is the competitive element so dominant or anxiety so strong as in time of war, for this situation calls into play every psychological and physical factor in the human make-up. It is in war that whole nations willingly submit themselves to the tribal God (often, paradoxically a deity of peace), and then deliberately set out to murder each other in the name of honour and justice. The concept of sacrifice is inseparable from warfare. The word itself rings out over the length and breadth of the land and tears and sweat, blood and toil become rallying cries of the community at bay.

The mascot, the charm, the talisman, are never more popular

than in wartime when they are enlisted for psychic defence. An old woman once told the author the secret of her survival in burning London during the air raids of the Second World War. "You hold your lucky stone with all your power and try to draw the luck out of it and into you." This type of power in a charm or amulet is known among the Polynesians as "mana", a spiritual force that can sometimes be found in stones.

Talismans were carried quite openly in battle down to the Thirty Years War, when they apparently went underground to re-emerge in times of crisis, as in the First World War, when the same ritual objects were found in the possession of German prisoners of war "having been handed down in country districts from one generation to another". Among British soldiers, as the *Daily Mail* of November 9th, 1916, reported, the most popular talisman of the First World War was the lucky penny. In the Second World War the luck-bringers or death-averting symbol became universal, for no soldier going into battle can fight effectively if he allows himself to brood upon the prospect of his own death. Every soldier imagines himself immortal, and even when he weakens he is often comforted by the superstition that he remains immune unless that one bullet "with his number on it" seeks him out. Often it is only the magical aid supplied by a talisman that can help to restore a declining faith in personal immortality. During both World Wars this type of luck-bringer became highly personalised, as if to establish a clearly defined psychic link with a loved one at home. Airmen in Britain and America tended to favour teddy bears and speckled neckties and their sweethearts' stockings. John Steinbeck, in his book *Once There was a War*, described graphically the feeling of collective unease that swept over an American bomber crew when one of their number lost his lucky charm, a medallion. In times of stress fear is infectious; usually the only defence is faith, and faith often requires reinforcement.

Even in times of peace the serviceman occupies an area of potential danger, for he is liable for battle at a moment's notice, and for this reason the superstitious side of his life always tends to be well to the fore. It is little realised that the ritual "wetting of stripes"—the token baptism of beer at the time of a serviceman's promotion—is based upon primitive libation and was known as long ago as the seventeenth century as "wetting one's pike".

The surviving superstitions of naval life are, as might be expected, very closely related to those of other seafarers. As with fishermen, certain words are tabooed by sailors, particularly the words "pig" and "rabbit", and actions symbolic of danger are studiously avoided, particularly in wartime. For a menstruating woman to sew on a sailor's badges is considered unlucky for menstruation, now as in the past, is associated with a curse, and indeed the "period" is often called "the curse". For an artist to paint a picture of a battleship is thought to seal its doom just as among savages a photograph was supposed to capture the subject's soul. Ill-fated ships are perhaps better known to the general public than unlucky machines on land, for the "jinx" ship is now a commonplace of news reporting. In the *Guardian* of January 22nd, 1969 there were banner headlines, "Fire aboard the aircraft carrier H.M.S. *Blake*, one of the most jinx-ridden ships in the Royal Navy".

The jinx sailor, or Jonah, as he is called, owes his nickname to the proverbially luckless Jonah of the Bible. His presence, needless to say, is unwelcome at sea. It is doubtful even whether the tattooing of a sailor's body, which is derived in part from a superstitious belief in the protective qualities of certain symbols, is proof against the true Jonah. American sailors believe, however, that pigs and cockerels tattooed to the left instep provide protection against drowning, while some individuals consider that tattooed designs on the body provide a safeguard against the pox. The superstitious aspect of naval tattooing (and for that matter all other types) is further emphasised by the popularity of luck-bringing symbols like the horseshoe, the black cat and the four-leaved clover.

There existed at one time a firmly held superstition among sailors that safety at sea could be assured if one took the precaution of touching one's sweetheart's pudenda for luck, a rite known as "touching the bun". Equally mysterious and still defying elucidation is the contemporary superstition in which girls touch a sailor's collar for luck whenever he heaves into sight.

The "crossing the line" ceremony represents one of the darker rites of primitive life at sea, for there is a distinct connection between the ritual shaving and bathing of the modern victim of this mock ordeal, and the ancient sacrifice of a member of the crew to the spirits of the waters.

Death at sea is, or was until recently, the occasion for a particularly macabre naval rite in which, prior to immersion when sewing up the body in its hammock, the last stitch was inserted through the nose of the corpse. This rite, strange to say, is found also among the

Eskimos who believe that it helps to keep the soul inside the body and that it also protects the corpse from attacks by wandering ghosts who might otherwise seek to possess it.

There is a close parallel between a ship in a state of mourning and a funeral on land. The ship, flying its flag at half mast, with yards scandalised and lowered, and booms dropped, is a nautical version of the sackcloth-and-ashes rituals of antiquity in which the garments of the mourners were rent and dishevelled.

An amusing example of the way in which a number of quite unconnected incidents can be telescoped and so give rise to a superstitious prejudice, cropped up in a case which recently came to the author's attention. It concerned a young soldier whose bad luck it was that the regimental goat died on the very day he joined his unit. From that moment onwards the soldier was regarded by his comrades as a jinx, and when at his first camp a storm broke out and all the tents collapsed his reputation as an ill-luck-bringer became established beyond all hope of redemption. He found it politic to leave the army as soon as possible, and apparently no obstacle was placed in his way.

Living animals symbolising the collective magic of a regiment or military unit were in all probability pets adopted in the first place by troops in situations of danger; having established themselves as luck-bringers they were retained afterwards as mascots. Looked at in this light, regimental mascots may be regarded as superstitious survivals. Among the best known examples of this interesting type of fetish are the regimental goat of the Royal Welch Regiment and the Irish wolfhound, the pride of the Irish Guards, both of which represent the idea of a spiritual link between animal and man.

In the Service funeral ceremony may be perceived rituals which had their origins in the superstitions of the ancient warrior castes. The presence of the horse, as at the military funeral of General Eisenhower, was based upon a primitive sacrificial rite in which the soldier's charger was ritually killed and buried with its master in order that it might serve him in the afterlife, while similarly the sword placed on the coffin was a relic of the custom of burying the warrior with his weapons. It is still customary to honour the dead at a Service funeral with three volleys; they are now fired in the name of the Trinity, but in pagan times they were a device for scaring devils from the corpse.

The traditional rites of Service life are disappearing apace, but one custom that survives is that in which a sergeant-major or officer serves morning tea to the private soldiers on Christmas morning, this being a relic of the Roman Saturnalia or feast celebrated in honour of the Golden Age of Liberty when Saturn ruled the world, and at which the slave was waited upon by his master. It has alas been nobody's business to document the history of these unconsidered trifles of service superstition; however, in the *Daily Mail* of November 30th, 1963, it was reported that an officer who had banned the traditional Christmas dinner in which the officers waited on the men, was completely within his rights "as there were now no general instructions". It was suggested at the time that the custom then was "at least forty years old and had probably originated in the trenches in the First World War". This is a custom which is hardly likely to become extinct as long as Service rank continues to exist. In Ulster during the Christmas of 1969, the officers were reported as taking over guard duty from the other ranks. The custom is said to have been adopted by the Royal Air Force shortly after its formation and is represented in the Royal Navy by the Christmas round of the ship carried out by a boy rating wearing the Captain's uniform.

The lucky charm has a long history among airmen. As long ago as the First World War the *Daily Mail* revealed that airmen, when touching wood for safety, were always careful to use living wood rather than dead wood, since the latter to their minds represented death. With the introduction of the eagle breast-badge on the airman's uniform, this symbolic bird at once became a luck-bringer and there was even some comment to the effect that it ought also to be displayed at the back of the uniform in order to provide psychic protection against attacks upon the rear of the plane. Airmen are selected for their emotional stability, but like everyone else they are driven to adopt the most amazing fetishes when under stress, a typical example being the wartime pilot who on arriving safely back at base after a successful bombing operation flings the entire contents of his pockets on to the turf as a thank-offering. Others have been known to kiss the ground on landing.

As might be expected, in both peace and war there is reluctance by most airmen to use danger-charged words like "crash". After a recent fatal accident at the Farnborough Air Show it became manifest that there existed in the other pilots a strong aversion to any suggestion that the dead pilot might have possibly been a victim of bad luck, for the obvious reason that none of the other entrants was prepared to face up to the prospect that this might be an unlucky day for all of them. As a result their conversation concentrated somewhat unsympathetically upon the victim's deficiencies as a pilot.

The organisation of man for power or for war has little in common with that of more peaceful or unadventurous pursuits. In the case of the one, anxiety and tension become the rule, but in the other one finds greater tranquillity punctuated by occasional points of tension when superstition has a tendency to come to the fore. To turn from the superstitious rites associated with government and its agents to the living folk customs of the community as a whole is in some respects a journey into the past, for our seasonal festivals belong properly to an agrarian economy that has long since been displaced by industrialisation. It is curious that so many of our older collective rites should have survived the revolutionary changes of the last two hundred years, for they have long ceased to have any truly functional role in social life. The reason might well be sought in the ingrained conservatism of the vast bulk of the population and its dislike of change, but perhaps even more so in the reverence most individuals tend to feel at some period of their lives for the vanishing past. Every industrialised society tends to look back sentimentally to the imaginary golden age of rural innocence, when magic and myth ruled a world untroubled by cruelty, greed or profit.

Many of the older rites, with their associated superstitions, have of course long since lost their meaning for the vast majority. May Day is a festival in which mankind once celebrated Earth's awakening from its winter sleep; it has become irrelevant, now, despite the efforts of modern folklorists to revive the old ceremonies. As far as the population as a whole is concerned there are no more than eight or nine occasions in the year which have any folk significance, these being New Year's Day, St. Valentine's Day, Shrove Tuesday, All Fools' Day, Easter, May Day, Halloween and Christmas, and they are often divorced from their original superstitious associations.

New Year's Day, representing the rebirth of the year, is considered particularly appropriate for the making of resolutions because it symbolises a new beginning, a fresh start, at a time when there is a kind of magic in the air. Everything that happens at New Year sets the pattern for the twelve months ahead, therefore it is essential to have money in the pocket, and a full stomach if one hopes to continue to be prosperous and well fed. The token coal, bread and money presented by the luck-bringer, or "first foot" as he enters the house on the stroke of midnight at New Year serve the same function, for they symbolise warmth, food and wealth.

If any superstitions associated with good and bad luck on St. Valentine's Day ever existed they must have long been forgotten, and likewise those of Shrove Tuesday, apart from the old belief that if one eats a pancake on this day one will have money all the year. All Fools' Day now has little that is associated with either good or bad luck, but Eastertide abounds with superstitions, perhaps appropriately since this festival was anciently associated with the spring equinox and sun worship. To wear new clothes on Easter Day, the time of renewal, brings luck throughout the year. In the Easter egg we still see a very obvious symbol of rebirth, and the lucky finder of a double yoke in an egg at Easter can expect a double ration of good fortune. This old pagan festival is a favourite among children, which is why the Easter egg has maintained its reputation as a kind of lucky charm. In some cases eggs are painted with coloured spots or dyed with onion skins, and in eastern Europe scarlet Easter eggs are planted in the fields to give magical protection against storms. At one time an egg would be placed beneath the plough before the first furrow was cut, as an aid to crop fertility. Hot cross buns crop up time and again among modern superstitions, arising from the old belief that bread baked on Good Friday possessed a magical quality. For this reason a hot cross bun, if kept throughout the year, will protect the household against not only fire but bad luck generally. Certain inns have preserved this pleasant rite, sometimes for decades on end.

Midsummer rites, like those of May Day, mean very little in modern life, although it is customary to hold Midsummer dances and balls, which are among the last surviving relics of the ancient festival of the summer solstice. A few genuine survivals of superstitious customs may still be found in out-of-the-way places, however. At the village of St. Cleer in Cornwall a Midsummer bonfire is lit and herbs and flowers cast into it as a device to offset the threat of any witch's spell, providing evidence that belief in the old-fashioned type of evil is still far from extinct in the West Country. This remains one of the traditional customs of St. John's Eve; it is intended to drive the Devil and his fiends out of community life. Equally venerable is the Beltane fire ritual performed at the Old Cross Kirk, Peebles, in mid-June, and regarded as one of the last of the ancient purifying fire festivals handed down from Celtic times. A ceremony with strong elements of tree worship is performed at Appleton in Cheshire each July, when there is dancing round a may-tree adorned with flowers; this is a survival of the old belief that certain trees possessed magically protective powers.

The coming of winter has always been associated with the return of the supernatural forces symbolising cold and death, for early November was a pagan feast of the dead and because of this many ceremonies of a purificatory nature were once performed at this time. Halloween is popularly supposed to be a most favourable time for the return of evil spirits, and although in terms of superstition the day means little to the modern city-dweller, there still exist a few survivals of the old ceremonies in rural life. In those parts of the country where Halloween customs continue to be observed, children will sometimes scoop out the insides of turnips to make lanterns shaped like grotesque human faces, or place a candle inside a scooped-out swede, thus recalling the long-forgotten festival of the dead.

There is still an annual ceremony of Turning the Devil's Stone at Shebbear in Devon, which is performed every November 5th in deference to the strong local belief that if this six feet by four feet by two feet stone—weighing over a ton—is left in the same position for two years running ill-fortune will fall upon the community. According to tradition the stone was dropped in its present position by the Devil; however, the more likely explanation is that it was originally associated with sun-worship. The rite is possibly one of the oldest in the British Isles.

Despite its associations with the Prince of Darkness the annual custom of tolling the Devil's knell at Dewsbury, Yorkshire, religiously observed each Christmas Eve, only originated in the fourteenth century, when a bell was presented to the church as an act of penance for the murder of the donor's servant. The tolling, it is now said, keeps the Devil from the parish for the whole of the ensuing year.

In our Christmas customs there can be seen a few strands of older forms of the magical beliefs once associated with Yule, an ancient feast of the dead. This is clearly indicated by the superstition that if one of the company at a Christmas gathering should cast a headless shadow in the firelight, he or she will die within the year. The Christmas pudding must always be stirred in a clockwise direction—this being the "way of the sun"—or ill luck will follow or the pudding be spoiled. The lucky sixpence or charm in the pudding brings good fortune to the one who finds it. Still strong among both young and old is the belief that it is unlucky not to take down

KATTERFELTO AND ONE OF HIS BLACK CATS
From a contemporary print

Katterfelto, a famous quack doctor, exploited the magic of black cats to enhance his reputation.

Rare picture of an Oriental wizard wearing lucky bone charms.

Christmas greenery *on* Twelfth Night or, worse still, that the house will become haunted by evil spirits for a whole year, a superstition harking back to the worship of the evergreen tree spirits of pre-Christian times which has recently been extended to include Christmas cards. In Yorkshire, however, there exists a custom in which a solitary sprig of mistletoe is kept for the whole year round and then replaced by another, for luck.

From the standpoint of superstition the vast majority of the folk rites that are practised today have little relevance to human need since they are no longer seriously regarded as protecting mankind against the forces of evil or of bringing to his aid the powers of good. Among such relics that are still to be found is the custom of well-dressing, which originated in the ancient worship of wells and streams. As symbols of phallic religion the upright pillar originally represented the male organ, and the well that of the female. For thousands of years wells were thought to be the abodes of spirits or gods, and in Wales almost until the present time certain wells were regarded as sacred, and stones were thrown into the water to discover what the future held. If the water bubbled it was a favourable omen but if it became clouded the outlook was ominous. It is interesting to see how this superstition has been revived in the twentieth century in the custom of throwing coins into artificial wishing-wells which are used for charitable fund-raising. On the islet of Eigg, off western Scotland there is an annual pilgrimage in April to St. Katherine's Well, famous for its healing properties. The approach to the well must always be made "dessil", that is from left to right, this being the course of the sun. This was originally a spell-creating rite performed by running round an object three times. In Scotland on May 5th pilgrimages are made to the Clootie Well near the battlefield of Culloden, where a coin is thrown into the waters as a tribute to the spirit of the well. A sip of water is taken as a potion to ward off evil, and a "clootie" or clout (piece of rag) is tied to the branches of the tree overhanging the water and left there until it rots.

There is a close connection between the present custom of wassailing the apple trees in Devon and Cornwall in January, when guns are fired through the branches, and the ceremonial driving off of evil spirits by means of fireworks and other explosions which is common in other lands.

Scotland still preserves the custom of honouring the Burry Man, dressed from head to foot in clinging burrs, as he silently makes his rounds through the town of South Queensferry each July immediately before the Ferry Fair. There is a strong belief in the locality that should he not be greeted wholeheartedly "bad luck will befall the house that is by-passed by the Burry Man". This ritual has continued for at least six hundred years, but its origins and meaning are lost in time.

Most spectacular of all our magical folk rites, however, is the annual ceremony of burning the Clavie, which is carried out at Burghead in Scotland each January 12th, the charred embers bringing good luck to whoever receives them.

In every sense most of these old customs may truly be said to represent superstitious survivals. There exist, however, a number of what might be called superstitious *revivals*, as for example the midsummer Druid rites at Stonehenge. This ceremony, which has been claimed to be of "unknown antiquity" is performed by a modern order of Druids at daybreak around the altar stone, and includes a prayer intoned at sunrise by one of their number dressed all in white. There can be little doubt that, so far as those present are concerned, sun-worship has the qualities of a living religion.

An extremely interesting revival is the lighting of a chain of bonfires which takes place in Cornwall on St. John's Eve; in its original form this was associated with the restoration of the powers of the dying sun. Furthermore there is a distinctly superstitious atmosphere about the service of dedication performed on this occasion, during which a sickle-shaped garland of flowers is committed to the fire, to the accompaniment of the chanting of this litany :

> In one bunch together bound
> Bonfire blossoms here are found
> Both good and ill.
> Thousandfold let good seed spring
> While ill-weeds fast withering
> This fire shall kill.

In assessing the validity of a superstition one has to bear in mind whether or not its observance or avoidance is seriously believed to attract good luck, and whether there exists a genuine apprehension of disaster if the rite is discontinued. In the West Country, incredible as it might seem, there can be found a few individuals who believe in all seriousness that if the Minehead hobby-horse ceremony on May Day were not to take place, the rising of the sun on that day would in some mysterious way be suspended. On the other hand very few of our modern folk-dancers can seriously believe that their particular performance has the slightest influence upon vegetation and crop growth.

The author has been amused to discover that superstition has now developed its own mystique and that some of the more dedicated enthusiasts are quite determined that the old magic shall never die. At Painswick, in furtherance of the old legend that only ninety-nine yew trees could ever flourish in the local churchyard, a local practical joker invariably administered a lethal dose of acid to the roots of every hundredth tree planted and by this means gave the tradition a renewed lease of life.

CHAPTER IX

PSYCHIC POWERS

IT IS customary to regard the exercise of what is commonly called psychic power as belonging to a different category from superstition, but as it will be seen, the two are closely related, and it might even be said that the former is a more fully developed version of the latter. On close examination it becomes apparent that the practices of groups organised for clairvoyance and magic are very similar to those observable in the superstitions of individuals. All are obviously founded upon certain basic principles of voice, touch, and gesture, as well as stylised symbolic relationships. There is, however, a qualitative difference between the two, in that collective superstitions tend to be positive and power-seeking, whereas the superstitions of individuals are in the main of a defensive character.

Clairvoyance has a great deal in common with certain forms of divination practised in classical times, notably crystalomancy which required the aid of a transparent object like a crystal globe, a pool of water or even a mirror. One still discovers the occasional spinster who stands hopefully before her mirror at midnight on Halloween in the hope of seeing the vision of her future husband, though this rite has tended to die out in recent times. Another form of clairvoyance closely associated with superstition is the interpretation of dreams, perhaps the most common of today's folk-practices, which was familiar to the ancient Greeks under the name of oneirocritica. There is yet another system, known as dactyliomancy, which is divination performed by means of a ring suspended on a fine thread over a round table, the edges of which are marked with the letters of the alphabet; the modern variant of this is the planchette of the spiritualists. Modern spiritualism also has much in common with ancient sciomancy, an art once employed for "calling up the names of the deceased to give the intelligence of things to come".

While it might be arguable whether or not clairvoyance and similar forms of psychic awareness ought properly to be classed as superstitions, there exists very good reason for suggesting that the majority of those who accept the existence of supernatural forces do so from what can only be described as a superstitious attitude. Most of those who regard clairvoyance as a genuine faculty, apparently base their beliefs upon an a priori conviction that there exist certain powers lying beyond the range of the five senses. Into this category come supernatural forms of communication which have entered the realms of psychic science under the name of extra-sensory perception, but which in the more earthy superstitions of the masses takes the form of divination from the burning or ringing of the ears. Without wishing to question the evidence put forward in support of such theories, it would be reasonable to concede that there must be some deep need to believe in these powers, for they appear not only as universal phenomena but show no sign of diminution with the advance of science.

The many cases that have been brought to the author's attention seem to indicate that a large number of individuals claim to undergo at some period in their lives experiences which can only be described as psychic. Sometimes clairvoyance takes place behind a façade of ritualism, as in the minor sorcery of teacup reading. In several cases it was discovered that the symbolism of the tea-leaves had very little, if anything, to do with the actual process of prediction, the eyes of the teacup reader being tightly closed throughout the process while the "future" presented itself in the form of a mental picture. It is obvious that in this type of "prediction" the tea-leaves themselves merely provide a focal point for the concentration of the seer, and a framework for the visionary process. One woman described to the author how useful chairvoyance had been to her in childhood, particularly in finding lost objects, but she felt that the faculty had declined as she grew older. The employment of clairvoyance for the discovery of "things that are stolen or lost" has been one of the primary functions of the seer from time immemorial.

A woman who used the crystal for daily guidance, though never professionally as she considered this to be detrimental to her powers, informed the author that before any vision appeared the whole interior of the crystal appeared as a series of whirling spirals of light, moving, as is invariable in such cases, in a left-right direction.

On the outskirts of London a woman who is the seventh daughter of a seventh daughter is still regarded with considerable awe by her neighbours because of her supposed ability to see into the future by means of a crystal. She has now discontinued this perfectly innocent activity, after being accused by her religiously-minded relatives of having dealings with the Devil.

Turning to organised clairvoyance, one discovers today a complex system of rites based upon certain fundamental principles of magic which are more commonly found in primitive superstitions. Up to twelve people sit in a spiritualist circle—never under any circumstance must it be thirteen. Where a trance medium is used, he or she becomes a vessel for the voice of the dead and the message is generally of an oracular nature. In psychometry an article is taken from one of those present, after having been carefully placed in an envelope to avoid contamination from other objects. The medium holds it in both hands and presses it to the forehead and with closed eyes interprets the message, which is apparently communicated by the agency of touch.

A stage is often reached in occult practices in which the emphasis shifts from the defensive to the offensive, ceasing to be directed towards the securing of protection against real or imagined dangers and taking a decisive step forward into deliberate attempts to control the environment. There are examples of people who believe it possible to compel the occurrence of events by will power alone. In October 1968 the journal *Pulse* described a case in which a man suffered grave injuries to his eyes from his habit of peering into the sun under the mistaken impression that he could thereby influence its power. Analogous to this is the belief in the effectiveness of the human will as an aggressive instrument. One woman of the author's acquaintance was so convinced that she possessed this power that she found it necessary to resist every hostile impulse for fear that a single random thought directed at an enemy might cause an unintended injury.

At this stage of emotional disturbance the subject is moving rapidly into witchcraft, but this is a situation which presents grave dangers for the individual, who risks the violation of a deeply implanted moral code, as by submitting, for example, to the atavistic urge to commit murder, if only of an imaginary kind. Many of those who indulge in evil thinking believe that malevolent thoughts and wishes will rebound upon the ill-wisher three-fold, and for this reason the amateur witch will often undergo a severe trauma if she gives way to this more melodramatic side of her nature. A girl who stuck pins into a photograph of a rival was so overcome when she discovered that her victim had suffered a road accident that she became ill herself from the shock. The magician of antiquity was extremely careful never to violate his moral code, particularly in view of the fact that any departure from the highest ethical standards was supposed to result in the loss of psychic power.

It is of particular interest to the student of latter-day magic that a very large number of apparently perfectly normal individuals will mark out a ritual circle with their hands as a form of psychic self-defence, and mutter little incantations to tranquillise their minds during those periods when they feel themselves under psychic attack.

There can be little doubt that amateur witchcraft, in the form of evil wishing, is as strong as ever it was in the past : perhaps, like envy, it can be regarded as inseparable from mankind. Anyone who appears in a television programme that deals with the supernatural usually receives phone calls and letters from people needing the services of a witch—sometimes enclosing tufts of hair and snippings of fingernails. One of the more bizarre examples in the author's collection was sent by a Cornish woman offering her old-age pension in return for the infliction of financial ruin upon a relative who she claimed had robbed her of a legacy. An impressionable young man from Lancashire was prepared to dedicate his whole life to the magical arts, while a prematurely bald Maltese threatened to use force if necessary if supernatural aid was not immediately forthcoming for the restoration of his hair. The author has even had callers seeking aid for the removal of voodoo spells, and, most dramatic of all, a midnight telephone request from a distraught woman to murder her employer by witchcraft.

As might be expected one occasionally comes upon some luckless individual who claims to be under a witch's spell. In cases of this type the sufferer has often passed through medical care with little amelioration of his or her condition. While writing this book the author, accompanied by witnesses, was approached by a woman who claimed to be under a gipsy witch's curse. She was obviously in an extreme state of emotional torment. Her sufferings arose, she insisted, from the fact that she had been compelled to exchange souls with the gipsy and that as a result her soul was now burning in Hell.

The gipsy fortune-teller is often responsible for the unscrupulous exploitation of the universal belief in the supernatural by encouraging the superstition that she has the power to cast a spell upon those who give her offence. The technique most commonly employed, however, and one which looked at logically is perfectly simple, demands that the potential customer be persuaded that she is suffering from the malice of some person unknown. She must then be talked into parting with good money in exchange for a blessing which is supposed to neutralise the spell. Those who have the temerity to resist the blandishments of the gipsy fortune-teller will often suffer agonies of uneasiness afterwards. One antidote employed by some housewives is to burn a snippet of their own hair in an open fire, or in a candle-flame, as this is supposed to cancel out the curse. The Vagrancy Acts of 1824 exist for the suppression of this type of menace.

While it is perfectly true to say that the superstitious beliefs of the coloured immigrants tend to be kept well in the background in their country of domicile, there are sufficient examples coming to light to suggest that the occasional ritual murder does indeed take place; while in some cases a very strong undercurrent of fear of witch-doctor power exists, especially among those originating from Africa. A case which recently came to the author's attention involved a young Malawi woman who had been persuaded that she had been placed under a spell by a witch in her homeland. In her frantic efforts to escape its influence she had paid several hundred pounds to a witch-doctor in Malawi, and when this failed had parted with the remainder of her money to certain so-called English seers who had charged her the sum of £10 for each prayer they offered on her behalf.

The secret power of these dangerous quacks of the superstition racket lies in the implantation of doubt in the mind of an already anxious victim, and then to relieve it by spurious assurances. The price the victim pays cannot be measured in money alone. Once trapped in the mesh of the fear of black magic the victim is too often condemned to a terrible, sometimes inescapable hell. The extent of what can only be described as the superstition racket is not fully known, but it is undoubtedly a serious social menace, for it battens upon the emotionally disturbed in every type of society, using psychological blackmail to extort thousands of pounds every year. Given an unscrupulous exploiter of the emotions and a distraught client, the task of moral blackmail is rendered relatively easy. The fortune-teller operates by means of what can only be described as a tipster technique, in which the failures rarely see the light of day, while the occasional successes are hailed to the very heavens. It is a lamentable fact of human nature that the client whose anxieties have been relieved is ready to broadcast the good news to the whole world, while the remainder maintain a shamefaced silence rather than betray to their friends an enslavement to superstitious fears. What is so terribly sad about many of the victims of the superstition-monger is that they so often need urgent medical help.

We are now living in a deeply superstitious age, perhaps inevitably so, since it is an age of anxiety. The ever-present fear of annihilation by the hydrogen bomb, the prevalence of violence, the sense of insecurity arising from rapid social changes, provide a favourable climate for a superstitious revival of an intensity unknown since the socially disturbed witch-fearing days of the seventeenth century.

The intense desire felt by so many for the acquisition of supernatural power can often lead to excesses which are not only socially troublesome but harmful to the subject's personality, because the more deeply involved one becomes in black magic and witchcraft the more likely one is to succumb to the powerful deep-seated fears of psychic attack that underlie one's personality.

Those who tend to scoff at the modern manifestations that pass under the name of occultism should consider that the mind of man, despite its modernistic furnishings, has probably remained structurally unchanged for thousands of years, and that in an environment in which magical beliefs become acceptable these "darker" aspects of human nature might well reassert themselves and become dominant. There undoubtedly exists a predisposition towards the supernatural in the human psyche and black magic is only old superstition writ large. It is in this light that one should consider the extraordinary manifestation that took place in London in the summer of 1968, when it was reported that "A community of young men and women professing a mock 'religion' of bizarre beliefs has established a chapter house in London. Among the group are those who claim to worship the Devil. . . . The cult is under the leadership of a black-bearded young man who describes himself as a Satanist." One of the rituals of this novel religion was the endearing habit of reeling off a litany of obscenities. These so-called Satanists, far from creating a new religion, are on the contrary the slaves of an extremely ancient one, based upon the superstition that it is possible to offset psychic attack by coming to terms with the powers of darkness through submission to them. More recently, a similar group was caught trying to restore the head of a slaughtered pig to life.

The morbid imagination of the masses can sometimes result in what in any other age would have seemed incredible. On Friday

March 13th, 1970 (an appropriate day in view of what follows), it was reported by newspapers that a vampire hunt had taken place in Highgate cemetery under the leadership of a "Mr Blood", during the course of which "something grey was seen moving slowly across the road". It had been the intention of these latter-day psychic researchers to stake the vampire through the heart with a wooden cross.

It is not generally realised that our modern black magic practices reflect the deeply implanted superstitious beliefs of people who apparently take for granted the existence of the Devil. Every year England sees a small number of churches and churchyards desecrated and the celebration of the black mass has become so commonplace as to cease to merit more than passing notice in the newspapers. The *Evening Standard* of November 1st, 1968, published a brief report headed, "Coffins dug up at witches' sabbath in a cemetery", which described a violation of graves in a North London churchyard, with crosses broken and corpses disinterred, one being found with a stake through its heart—to quote : "Through the coffin had been plunged an iron stake in the form of a cross." The fanatics who perpetrated this outrage were carrying out the rites of one of our most ancient superstitions, that called necromancy, which was based upon an imagined power to communicate with the spirits of the dead by means of their disinterred bodies.

The most notorious series of outrages of this type, however, will always be associated with the village of Clophill in Bedfordshire, where the disturbance of graves has been continuous over a period of at least seven years, and where in the present year several skulls have been disinterred.

The group practice of supernatural rites has always been one of the normal manifestations of human behaviour, for it incorporates at one end of the scale our unorthodox religions, and at the other, certain fringe cults covered by the general term mysticism and occultism. The appeal of the supernatural is likely to remain strong while people continue to believe that there exist outside of the human personality certain cosmic powers, sometimes friendly but mainly hostile, with which mankind has to come to terms. These are precisely the *same* forces which the average individual has in mind when he reacts to the dangers of tempting providence by crossing his fingers or touching wood. An extremely interesting example of a modern superstitious cult has become fashionable under the name of The Witch Cult, which must be distinguished from black magic and which, despite its claim to an ancient lineage, is in all probability very modern in origin.

Modern witchcraft is worthy of special study not only because of the way in which it has successfully adapted a vast range of obsolete religions and superstitious practices to its needs, but for the manner in which it has succeeeded in attracting the interest of ever-growing numbers of people, mainly from among the young. It is quite immaterial that the claim of the witches to be the spiritual and lineal descendants of sorcerers of the Middle Ages is unsupported by historical evidence. Of infinitely greater importance is the character of the beliefs to which they adhere.

Today's witchcraft was almost certainly initiated in 1951 by the late Dr. Gerald Gardner, a scholarly showman, who taking advantage of the repeal of the Witchcraft Act in that year, became virtually the high priest of witchcraft as well as its public relations officer on television. The new seed fell upon fertile soil, for magical beliefs had long been encouraged by a lurid type of fiction and within a very few years the new movement became several hundreds strong, organised in "covens" up and down the country. From the writings of Dr. Gardner and some of his followers it has been possible to gain some measure of the skill with which the witches managed to present an entirely new movement in the guise of an old one, and at the same time to cloak the most primitive superstitious beliefs with a pseudo-scientific terminology. The witchcraft newspaper *Pentagram* of December 5th, 1965, described the process by which the so-called magical power is generated: "Basically the dance pattern is supposed to set up rhythmic resonances in the dancers themselves so that their whole beings respond to and reproduce that particular frequency wave form in the ethnic inner-world. As their physical bodies act so should their inner existence harmonise and produce reactive effects which were once called 'magical'."

A hand-book containing the rituals, passwords and initiation ceremonies of this movement is in existence and provides a clear indication of the manner by which the witches have succeeded in elevating the basic superstitions to which all humanity is heir to a pseudo-religious cult. The "Eightfold Paths or Ways to the Centre" describes the process by which the environment can be compelled to submit to the human will, and the "astral body" be projected from its physical shell. Incense and drugs are recommended for the release of "the spirits", and power is not merely generated by means

In America and Scotland to carry a spade within doors "brings death into the house."

A falling picture is an omen of death.

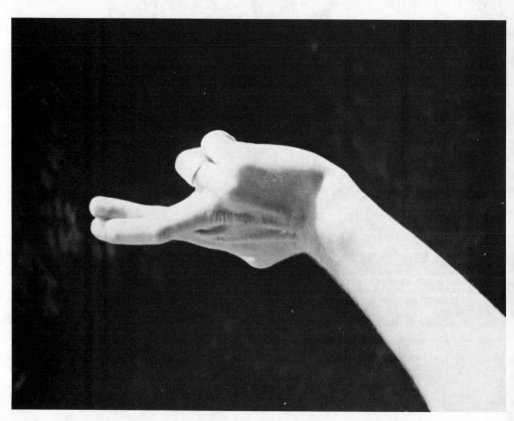

To offset bad luck—make the sign of the cross.

of the ritual dance, but by the control of the breath and blood. Inevitably, perhaps, modern witchcraft engages in a number of eccentric sexual practices, including ritual intercourse, which is euphemistically described in the manual as "The Great Rite". It is also apparently evincing authoritarian tendencies, for there now exists a "King of the Witches".

A re-affirmation of certain basic principles of superstitious belief may be seen when witches perform their dances in the left-to-right or clockwise direction, which is considered essential if the magic is to be of a social or helpful kind. There are, however, certain occasions when the witch reverses the process, but this is not to be undertaken lightly since evil spells must be paid for in terms of some forfeiture or loss. Many witches believe that black magic rebounds threefold upon the spellbinder. Underlying the creed of the witches may be detected the ordinary superstitious beliefs of the layman, for the witch is wholly involved with the problem of attracting the good spirits and with warding off psychic attacks.

Collective witchcraft is not to be recommended as a form of psychotherapy, as there exists the constant danger that the practitioner who becomes too deeply entangled in this artificial world of self-induced wish-fulfilment may become so divorced from reality as to be almost demented. There are many cases on record in which the light-hearted entrant into a coven has left it with a nervous breakdown.

To sum up the dangers of modern witchcraft is extremely difficult, since the sincerity of the vast majority of its participants cannot be in doubt; nevertheless it should be avoided if only for the fact that a number of vicious exploiters may be found within its ranks. Cynical though the observation might be, it is at least a tenable proposition that in terms of superstition the danger arises not so much because our modern witches claim the power to bewitch others as that they are themselves bewitched. As far as the British Isles are concerned, witchcraft and magic have now been placed almost upon an institutional basis, and it is now more than a rationalist's life is worth to deny the reality of supernatural powers. Gone are the days when superstition presented itself in a shame-faced manner and when sorcery was regarded as no more than an amusing eccentricity. In those areas of the country once associated with the older rural witchcraft there has recently been an amazing revival of interest in the subject. The small Essex village of Canewdon, with its legend that as long as the church tower stands there will be seven witches in residence, and that each time a stone falls from the tower one witch will die and another will take her place, has seen a resurgence of the belief which is now, if anything, even stronger than in the past. The life of the community has changed, the old farm labourers have been replaced by Londoners, but still the superstition survives on its old site as it has continued to do for the last thousand years.

Even his Satanic Majesty himself might be tempted to chortle at the latest manifestation taken by superstitious mania in the British Isles. A factory has recently been set up in the Home Counties for the express manufacture of witchcraft equipment, including magical swords and daggers, and furthermore planchettes are now on sale in the toyshops. As if this were not enough, and in order to be in at the death so to speak, it is now possible to purchase a pop-art tomb of perspex and plastic, this being part of the British "Death is good for you" campaign. Finally, the illustrious owners of the nation's haunted houses, capitalising upon the revival of interest in the supernatural, have set up what can only be described as a "stately ghosts industry" for the express purpose of luring dollars from coach-loads of gullible and extremely superstitious American tourists.

CHAPTER X

AMERICAN SCENE

THE REMARK that Nature has the habit of taking vengeance upon those who presume upon her bounty, which itself might almost rank as a superstition, is particularly true of the United States, where the most rampant superstitions manage to exist together with the most dynamic social economy the world has ever known. Here man has set aside moral considerations in his passion for mastery over the forces of nature; hence in a land of plenty there is starvation, insecurity and continuing anxiety.

Among the socially disinherited the older type of lore continues to flourish relatively unchanged, but in the higher social echelons where competition for the bare essentials of life has been replaced by the rat-race for economic privilege and power the role of the supernatural is very strong. It can be seen expressed very clearly in the social doctrines by which the American economy directs its policies.

The folklore of capitalism incorporates a number of economic and social myths that are no more than old superstitions. Terror of the new encourages a tendency to decry unfamiliar social policies in terms that are borrowed from demonology. As Thurman Arnold wrote in his *Folklore of Capitalism* : "When men are confronted with the choice between the myth and the reality they have only two courses. The first is ceremony drums and oratory; the second is reason and dialectic," and he continued : "The true faith is Capitalism, its priests are the lawyers and economists. The Devil consists of an abstract man called a demagogue." More recently this same Devil has worn the scarlet livery of the communist.

When beleaguered, economic man tends to take refuge behind tribal symbols which provide for him a supernatural barrier against the enemy whosoever and whatsoever it might happen to be at the time. He also evinces an over-riding tendency to consult the tribal witch-doctor who alone has the inherited power to read the stars. In this situation the economic pundit fulfils precisely the same role as the old-time prophet and all men harken and marvel at his words. As

Richard Lewinstein pointed out in his book *Prophecy and Predictions*: "... the history of prophecy from Babylon to Wall Street is an unbroken saga of man's struggle to peer into the future and to adjust his personal and social life to suit what he imagines to be his own interests". Of the prophets themselves he wrote: "As a rule the prophets were patriotic and enterprising men who lent their masters courage." This might indeed have been the case on rare occasions but it is equally true that the prophet's oracular pronouncement was cleverly designed to be capable of a number of often quite contradictory interpretations, in deference to the primary objective of the operation which was the furtherance of the prophet's own interests rather than those of his client.

The business cycle, as this same author lucidly explains, is a concept belonging equally to mythology and bears comparison with ancient augury or the divination of the future from the entrails of animals, as was practised in classical times. In modern America, for example, there apparently exists a branch of the Stock Exchange that specialises in statistical divinations which are in essence very similar to those of the soothsayers.

The ruling impulse of all social orders is to secure protection against the intrusion of social dangers, hence the passion for underwriting the future by taking out insurances in which the policy itself becomes the modern talisman. Man has also created a number of economic fetishes which have little or no relevance to reality, one being the myth of progress and the other the inevitability of boom and slump. Men who invest their whole futures in a market economy are, whether they like it or not, doomed to develop a gambling mentality, and gamblers are the most illusion-ridden, superstition-bitten fall-guys in the world. It is for this reason that many businessmen studiously avoid starting new ventures on Fridays, and more than a few carry some lucky charm or mascot in their pockets.

An attitude of mind not at all uncommon among businessmen who have been beaten to the post in a deal is a refusal to concede that the successful rival has been cleverer than they are themselves. Instead they will declare him to be "star born", or an inherently luckier individual. This device not only preserves their own sense of inviolability but provides an effective antidote to the pangs of jealousy.

The supernatural also plays its part in the minor politics of commercial life, with an occasional reversion to divinatory practices of the most primitive kind, as when in 1968 the Junior Chamber of Commerce of Marksville, Louisiana, organised a frog-jumping contest, each amphibian bearing the name of a Presidential candidate. The winner of the contest, a frog with the name of the Alabama segregationalist Governor George Wallace, has, however, yet to be elected President of the United States.

Among American businessmen boasting is usually avoided like the plague, especially by those whose activities depend to a great extent upon the so-called "laws of chance", and it is not unknown for the stock market speculators, like the gambler of Monte Carlo, to touch surreptitiously the back of any hunchback in the vicinity before embarking upon a particularly hazardous speculation. Lower down in the economic hierarchy the element of superstition is so closely linked with the risk situation that a cautious salesman will often continue to wear a cravat or some other article of clothing that has become associated in his mind with a successful deal, thus transforming it into insurance for further success. It is not at all uncommon for a plastic horseshoe to be included in a case of samples, and it is customary also for a floral horseshoe to be presented to a shopkeeper when he opens new premises for the first time. A salesman faced with a run of bad luck will often attempt to change his circumstances by a ritual change of clothing or even by taking a special bath for the occasion.

Among Latins in the United States there exists a tendency to blame loss of trade upon the evil eye of some competitor, a disaster which incidentally can always be offset by the discreet burning of cloves. American labour relations are equally subject to supernatural forces, and in one case a renowned expert in inflicting the baleful glance of the evil eye was employed to intimidate any individual in the factory who tended to be slack at his job.

As one would expect, American industry can be as jinx-ridden as its Old World counterpart, for industrial and workshop superstitions are cast in the same mould the world over, but with local variations representing either a further stage in the evolution of the superstition itself or a "fossilised" survival from the past. Thus in American ship-building a silver coin is often placed beneath the mast, but in laying the cornerstone of a new building an apparently new superstition exists to the effect that a woman who witnesses this inaugural ceremony will not marry for a year, the closest parallel to this being the Old World rural superstition which declares that the woman who cuts the first sheaf of the harvest may hope to marry within the year.

The completion of any structure has always been regarded as a challenge to the gods of chance and this is responsible for the lingering belief that the final brick in a building should never be put in place since this may result in some destruction or damage to the fabric. Originally such an action would have been regarded equally as exposing the new house to the intrusion of hostile spirits.

In America there long existed an industrial superstition which was associated in its original form with treasure-seekers of the Old World, where hoards of gold and silver had been found from time immemorial in the tumuli of the ancient Sea Kings. The treasures of the Americas, however, took the form of oil and this, by a process of analogy, led the oil-digger to the graveyard, the United States' equivalent of the tumulus. The nineteenth-century oil-smeller, or "doodlebug" to use his nickname, with his dowsing rod was a familiar figure in American cemeteries during the search for oil. Professional "water witches" continue to be an integral part of social life in some parts of rural United States, and have even been employed by cotton growers to discover underground streams. Using his forked stick, which reacts directly it makes contact with water, the dowser occupies a halfway position between the old-time magician and the modern scientist.

It is not too surprising to discover the remnants of some very old superstitious attitudes among modern American workmen. Men in the steel industry, whose work involves hazardous climbs, will sometimes twist their braces before commencing work, but whether this, like knotting a handkerchief, is a reminder of the need to take care or whether on the other hand it is based on the old superstition that a knot secures good luck, is difficult to say.

The more common domestic superstitions of the United States require no more than passing mention since they have been discussed at length in the earlier part of the book. As one might expect, there exist fears of the consequences of walking under a ladder, of spilling salt, of tempting providence by audacious boasting and so on and so forth. What is of particular interest in the American scene, however, is the many varied forms of specifically New World folklore, which serve as a reminder that superstitions rarely stand still but move with the times or, on the other hand, become modified by local circumstance.

Instead of teacup reading the Americans, as might be expected of a nation of coffee drinkers, utilise their own national beverage for divinatory purposes, the system employed being one that has close affinities with the Old World tradition of water divination, in which the shape of the future is determined by examining the bubbles in a well or spring. In the American coffee-cup rite the bubbles that float towards you indicate money to come, while those which move in the other direction signify that money will be lost. The same motif may be observed in the folded money superstition. By folding a note towards you, more notes are attracted to you; reverse the process and your money flows in the other direction.

Very close to the familiar Old World falling picture superstition is the current American belief that if a portrait is turned upside down disaster will descend upon the head of the subject portrayed. Yet, at the same time, there is a curious reversal of the European umbrella superstition in the belief that by *not* carrying an umbrella one ensures fine weather, as if to suggest that the umbrella plays the part of a magic wand having an innate power to attract rain.

In some respects American folk beliefs may be seen as a museum of superstitious concepts which have somehow managed to survive the winds of change relatively intact. There are those who believe it unlucky to turn over in bed and others who have redefined in pseudo-scientific terms the old doctrine that to get out of the wrong side of the bed in the morning brings bad luck, by declaring that the left side attracts hostile and the right friendly influences which are connected in some mysterious manner with the magnetic poles. In New England one is careful not to rock an empty chair since this brings death into the family, whereas in old England to rock an empty cradle meant the arrival of a new baby. Even the superstitions associated with mirror-breaking appear in America to possess their own distinctive characteristics, for there the *deliberate* breaking of a mirror has no ill effects, while even the consequences of an accidental breakage can be averted if one is lucky enough to find a five-dollar bill and at the same time remembers to make the sign of the cross. The five-dollar bill has apparently inherited some of the qualities originally associated with the gold piece, long regarded as a luck-bringer in old-time America, and it is very possible that the latter originally derived its virtues in turn from the gold nugget which, in American pioneer days, was carried in the pocket of the gold-miner as a lucky charm.

Certain fortuitous events are regarded as happy auspices; thus to pick up a safety pin in the New World is as lucky as it is to pick up an ordinary pin in England. A ladder with an odd number of rungs is as lucky to the one who climbs it as it is unlucky for the one who walks beneath it, or any other type of ladder for that matter.

Clothing, as one would expect, assumes a prominent role in the saga of American superstitions. To burn a hole in a dress indicates that one is being lied about, in exactly the same way that burning ears are everywhere supposed to be a sign that one is being discussed. An American variant of the Old World custom of heralding the spring by buying new clothes at Eastertide is the belief that to be lucky an American woman must wear three new things on Easter Day.

On the principle: change the method, change the luck, it is customary when jewellery is restyled to adhere to the original design as far as possible if the luck is to be preserved.

The common belief that "disasters always happen in threes" has its American equivalent in the superstition that "fires follow fires". The English superstition that it is unlucky to see a nun has its parallel in the United States' belief that it is unlucky to see a nunnery. For letters to cross in the mail is a sign of misfortune, since the cross in this case represents, fairly obviously perhaps, the crossing or frustration of desires. What is apparently a twentieth-century superstition holds that a girl who spills her face powder will quarrel with her friend. In this case no doubt the powder, like dust, is equated with luck, and its fall becomes logically the symbol of misfortune.

In the United States, eyebrows that meet across the nose are supposed to be a sign of wealth; in the older belief once common in Europe, such a sign was regarded as evidence of the evil eye.

Whatever the original source of touching or knocking on wood as a superstition (and some have even considered it to be a fairly modern substitution of the older rite of touching cold iron for luck), there is not the slightest doubt that it has become firmly implanted in the modern way of life, being the most commonly used prophylactic against the evil consequences of presuming upon fortune. America's physicians have even noted the habit of certain patients of replying to the question: "How are you?" with a cautious: "All right so far", followed by a ritual knock on wood.

Some amazing hair superstitions live on with unexpected vigour in the United States. Thus, to cure baldness, men will shave the head very closely, while many believe it necessary to singe the hair after cutting in order to retain its "vital fluid". Loss of hair in both the Old World and the New is frequently said to result from an overtight hatband, and here and there one may find the lurking fear that evil spirits can make their entry into the body via the hairs of the head. One of the common heritages of both European and American folklore insists that it is useless to pull out a grey hair since ten more will grow in its place. Those blessed with a luxuriant growth of hair on the arms are, according to the same type of theorist, destined to make money.

If Europe has been the home of lost causes, then America certainly justifies the description of being the experimenters' paradise. Innumerable are the pseudo-scientific cults that have found congenial soil in American life. Blue glass mania was at one period the rage, as was the cult of magnetism with its ever-potent electromagnetic belts. Terms like "Odic force" and "N" Rays streak like rockets across the intellectual sky and vanish over the horizon, destined to re-emerge disguised as novelties in a generation's time. Mystical cults have an apparently irresistible appeal to the American as perhaps nowhere else in the world. There still exists, to take just one example, the Koreshanity Church in Chicago with its 5,000 followers who firmly believe that the universe is a hollow sphere with the earth at its centre.

The superstitions of health continue to play a very active part in the beliefs of the American poor. Growing pains are often taken for granted, as is the belief that red string tied around any part of the body afflicted with rheumatism will relieve pain, while cotton thread is useful for cramp if tied round the ankle.

Many of the superstitions of American life, particularly those of the so-called medical "fringe", are representative of mankind's oldest health techniques. Like the folk-healer in the darkest corners of rural Europe, the Californian "practitioner" will often diagnose ailments and select his remedies by aid of the pendulum. As in the medieval past, a vast industry is now dedicated to the cure of impotence by means of love philtres or potions which include the famous Philadelphia love powders and lodestones which are supposed to attract love by magnetism, and there is even in existence a Lovers' Cook Book. Aphrodisiac foods are marketed on an ever greater scale, the underlying principle being nothing more nor less than white magic; however, there can be no doubt that in terms of suggestion an aphrodisiac will sometimes prove effective, but only so long as it is confined to stimulating the imagination. Some aphrodisiacs if taken internally can produce at best a stomach ache and at worst an extremely painful death.

Many interesting relics of love magic may be found among American youth of the less sophisticated kind. Divination occurs in the form of the rite which says that if a girl stands at the roadside and counts ten red automobiles and then looks for a red-headed girl wearing a purple dress, and then a man with a green tie, the next elegible young man who speaks to her is destined to be her husband. Apparently the influence of the old superstition :

> Change the name but not the letter,
> Marry for worse instead of better

has led to the refusal of many American girls to marry a man whose surname bears the same initial as their own.

Some American love superstitions stand out particularly. If an English spinster takes the last slice of bread from the tea table it means that she will "have a handsome husband and ten thousand a year", but in the United States it is the bachelor who can expect this bonus from fate. Some of the sexual beliefs current in modern America almost defy credibility. Blondes are considered not only dumb but far more inclined to sexual intercourse than brunettes, and red-headed girls even more so. Some of the oldest myths in circulation point apparently to a survival of the ancient taboo against menstruating women. It is held, for example, that intercourse during a woman's period can lead to baldness in the male, or even impotence. Even more exotic is the belief that hormone treatment can increase the size of the sexual organs.

Whether the curious devices sometimes employed by many American girls to offset pregnancy are superstitious in origin, is hard to say, but even as examples of the older style of popular error they provide evidence that some bizarre beliefs can be handed down from mother to daughter, or transmitted from girl friend to girl friend. Thus today we have the Coco-Cola douche, in which many American girls have absolute faith, since it is said to be more effective a contraceptive than old-time soap and water. This is also apparently a modern variant of the old-time specific "hot bath and hot gin" for pregnancy.

American birth superstitions have much in common with those of the Old World but with certain special variations of their own. If an unborn child kicks on the right side of the womb it is a sign that it is a boy, but if on the left it is a girl. In Iowa, so the author learns, as no doubt in other places, the pendulum is sometimes used to determine the sex of an unborn baby.

The superstitions of death follow the general European pattern, "no death without a warning" being still an accepted article of faith, and there exists also a strong feeling that a grave must be dug facing the east in order to face the direction from which Gabriel is expected to blow his horn on Judgement Day. Another American death superstition insists that a drowned woman floats face upwards, whereas a drowned man floats face downwards.

American ghosts, it would appear from all the available evidence, tend to be somewhat noisy characters, exhibiting a backwoodsman indifference to the refinements of the art of haunting. In common with their opposite numbers in Europe they have a strong tendency to loiter in graveyards at night and to avoid lighted candles like the plague.

The American scene contains within its encyclopedic catalogue of odd beliefs some amusing eccentricities. In deference to the fact that the mind continues to work during sleep, students will often place their text books beneath their pillows so that instruction can continue over-night.

American waiters, doubtless as the result of bitter experience, have decided that if a customer selects a seat other than the one allocated to him it is a certain sign that the tip he gives will be a poor one. A one-armed guest, possibly because such a person finds it difficult to reach his pockets, is ominous of a very poor tip. Oddly enough it is unlucky for a waiter to receive a tip early in the day since this suggests that the day is unlikely to be profitable for him.

An element of old-style magical beliefs can also be detected in the lore of the American in the street. Among devices generally employed to attract luck are giving coins to a beggar, and carrying a doll as a mascot or, when intending to drink from a fountain, being careful to approach it from a left-to-right—"sunwise"—direction.

Most of the more general types of superstition represent variations of either the European-style luck-attracter, or the ill-luck deterrent, although the really potent magical devices are rarely revealed since even to speak of them destroys their power. Who for example would recognise in the habit of carrying a Bible a latter-day device for protection against the evil eye? In the Second World War American servicemen actually carried steel-bound Bibles in their pockets to deflect enemy bullets. Even a holy man can on occasion be promoted to serve as a lucky charm, as in the present Vietnamese War when the status of a protective saint was influenced to a considerable extent by successes or failures in battle. It was probably for this reason that paratroop units began to wear the St. Christopher medallion in place of that of their traditional protector, St. Michael.

The superstitions associated with American sporting life are intricately bound up with the risk factor; therefore, the more competitive the game the more likely will it be for superstitions to take root. Baseball players imagine that by the simple process of rubbing the head of a Negro bellboy they can lure fortune in their direction, and the statue at West Point is always given a ceremonial rubbing before a match begins. At a certain Naval Academy coins are thrown into the fountain before a ball game, doubtless to conjure up the support of the in-dwelling water spirit. In baseball it is sometimes thought that a left-handed pitcher brings luck to his team. And it is well known that a certain baseball player wears the same lucky vest in every game he plays. In a recent interview with golf professionals it was discovered that nearly 25 per cent were superstitious. Magic apparently lurks in the more obscure corners of every golfer's life. It seems that a young woman who took an excessive number of putts in a competition in 1969 was presented with a "hex symbol" by her well-wishers, this being described as "a medallion inscribed with a bird which is normally painted on the barn doors by Middle West farmers to give them a good crop". Generally a metal disc carried in the pocket of a golfer is considered to be perfectly adequate as a luck-bringer, although a large number of players tend to be superstitious also about the colour of the clothes they wear.

It is one of the virtues of American superstition that so many antidotes to misfortune have been preserved. Elsewhere, as in the British Isles, few remedies exist apart from the time-honoured touching wood, crossing fingers, or the proverbial "bless you" following a sneeze. The American cursed with an unlucky break at cards, and recognising that he is under psychic attack has only to snap his fingers, this being the oldest method known of banishing any evil spirits. Annexed to the old superstition that it is unlucky for two friends to wash in the same water is the antidote, if both parties make the sign of the cross with their thumbs all will be well. This doubtless applies in the case of the analogous superstition which declares it to be unlucky for two people to wipe their hands on the same towel.

The American theatre, as one would expect, is as elsewhere the centre of a vast wealth of protective lore, every actor having his own individual system for luck-bringing or danger-avoidance. Even the most casual reference to the catchword of a play is ominous; peacocks' feathers are hazardous; and inevitably the performance of *Macbeth* is pregnant with disastrous possibilities. In America there exists a belief not generally found elsewhere, which regards carrying a make-up box by an actor or actress as ominous of misfortune. There are all kinds of other eccentricities. To wear a wig, for example, is lucky, and artificial flowers on stage are luckier than live ones for the reason that should a petal fall a performer may fall likewise. On the other hand if an actor accidentally falls on stage it is a sign of continuous work, since a fall in a theatrical context symbolises the opposite in real life. There exist jinx theatres which have an unhappy reputation for particular actors, who tend therefore in consequence never to describe them by their proper name. Knitting on stage is psychically dangerous, and it is ominous if a cat happens to walk across the stage during rehearsals.

The advance of technology has had precious little influence upon American superstitions other than to re-establish them in new situations. Thus in a taxi-driver's cab a pair of miniature baby shoes will serve as a lucky mascot and, as in the United Kingdom, washing a car invites rain the next day. Many racing motorists have a strong objection to having a woman in the pits, since a female represents the negative or unlucky principle in life. Airmen cross unused seat-belts before taking off, dominated by precisely the same superstitious fear of the unknown that prompts the steel-worker to twist his braces. Others have been known to spit on the wheels.

Moving to the latest realms of technological advance we have astronauts wearing special colours when preparing for long space flights, and others who regard a perfect rehearsal in this sphere as ominous as it would be in the theatre. The disaster to Apollo 13 is hardly likely to reduce the impact of the unlucky thirteen superstition. Among new superstitions we find the belief that space flight and H-bomb tests disturb the weather, and that computers are feminine. Everyone apparently hates the computer (which is condemned as a kind of mechanical devil) and delights in its mistakes and falls from grace. Perhaps the most deeply implanted of all the modern American myths is the growing belief in Unidentified Flying Objects, which has begun to acquire almost the status of a religion, so much so that to express doubts as to the authenticity of these intruders from outer space has become something of a heresy. One is strongly tempted to make comparisons between the mythology of the U.F.O.s with that of the original messengers from space—the birds—who were so long regarded as the agents of the gods, the spirits of prophecy and the revealers of hidden truths, and who in some mythologies were actually believed to be the offsprings of the sun and moon.

America, perhaps needless to say, has created not only a cult of superstition but a superstitious cult in its National Society of Thirteen against Superstition, Prejudice and Fear which meets on Friday the 13th. The state of Missouri, not to be outdone, has instituted its own Lucky 13 Club, but despite all this the influence of fearful superstitions in American life can be expected to continue exactly as before.

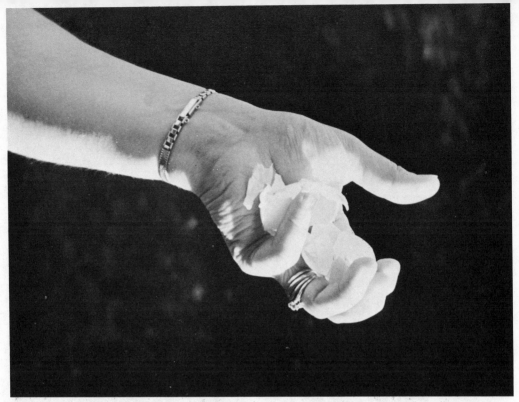

Old superstition—if you unthinkingly crush an eggshell you may end a sailor's life.

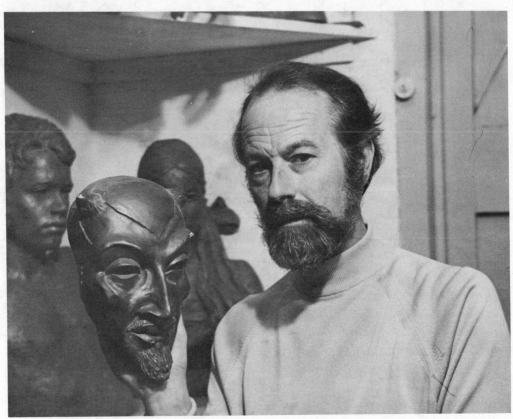

Richard Browne, F.R.B.S., with a "lucky devil" (a present from a friend).

Wash down the car and it's sure to rain—a very modern Anglo-Ameri-can superstition.

CHAPTER IX

REGIONAL AMERICA

REGIONAL AMERICA is a great watershed of superstitious beliefs, a veritable treasure-house for the folklorist searching for the grass roots of ancient traditions. The contribution of the English, Germans Dutch, Spanish and Italians to American occult lore has been immense, for together with their more materialistic culture the immigrants imported the magical beliefs of their European homelands, the legends, the ghost stories, the folk rites and, above all, the superstitions. There can be little doubt that a visitor to New England a century ago would have found the fabric of Anglo-Saxon belief relatively intact, but much of this has since become diffused as the result of further immigration. Those later arrivals the Irish have made their own distinctive contribution to New World culture, one example being the introduction of the Old-World Halloween celebration, a paganistic rite which would have been condemned as blasphemous by the Puritans who preceded them.

The private and collective superstitions still surviving in New England are recognisably a part of the Anglo-Saxon heritage. A letter received by the author from a friend in Massachusetts describes a number of clearly defined English superstitions almost untouched by the passage of the years and the change in locale. The magical property of the ordinary pin is reflected in the poetic maxim :

> See a pin and pick it up
> And all day you'll have good luck.
> See a pin, let it lay,
> Bad luck you'll have all the day.

There are a number of variations from the Anglo-Saxon tradition, however, most of them of a minor character, as in the following warning against presuming upon the future. In old England one would say : "Sing before breakfast, cry before supper", but in New England the word "night" has been substituted for "supper". Certain superstitions have a familiar ring, like "Never open an umbrella inside a house", but others have long been forgotten in England, if indeed they were ever known there, as for example "Never lay a hat on a bed", which has much in common with the English prejudice against placing a pair of unused shoes on a table.

The old taboo on the holy day or day of rest is reflected in the maxim, "Never make plans on a Sunday". In the British Isles one finds a still strong belief in the quite unfounded statement that an agreement transacted on the Sabbath is without legal validity.

Once again one discovers the ritual magic of touching wood as a device employed to offset the dangers of over-optimism.

The dual role of the black cat as both a good and bad luck bringer (a confusion that has never been satisfactorily cleared up) is borne out in the New England superstition that when a black cat crosses your path you must cross your fingers if you wish to offset trouble.

If two people utter the same word simultaneously, obviously a sign of psychic intervention, the situation demands that they also recite simultaneously :

> What goes up the window, smoke.
> May your word and my word never be broke.

and their wishes will (it is hoped) come true. In England it is usual for both parties to link little fingers and repeat the name of a poet.

The people of the savannah, deep in the Okenfenokee swamp, many of whom are supposed to have originated in the settlement founded by General Oglethorpe, include many of French Huguenot, Spanish, and Scots Irish stock, with the result that there has developed a curious amalgam of superstitious beliefs. There still exist, however, among the Okenfenokee many individuals of pure Anglo-Saxon origins whose outlook towards life up to until little more than a generation or so ago belonged rather to the eighteenth century than to the twentieth and whose surviving superstitions are quite archetypal, being well described as "almost Elizabethan". It was not unknown for love magic of a primitive type to be practised, one ingredient being "white moss from the skull of a murdered man". This curious and nauseating prescription, called in seventeenth-century England "usnea", once had many medicinal and magical uses. The superstition arose in the first place from the primitive belief that any individual whose life had been prematurely terminated retained an unexhausted quantity of life force within his body which might be drawn upon for therapeutic purposes or even for love magic.

There also existed certain forms of magic which could deflect bad luck and attract good luck and compel the spirits of fertility to submit to human desires. A lodestone from a deer worn as an amulet "gave the power to produce twins at will", and an eagle-stone "taken from the living bird" was a charm which secured faithfulness in both husband and wife. A form of bewitchment similar to the European Witch Bottle was employed to compel the return of a faithless lover. In this case the contents, which included "seven hairs from a black cat, seven scales from a rattlesnake and seven bits of feather from an owl", were burned for seven minutes on a fire together with hairs and nail-parings, and the hoped-for result was the production of seven agonising pains in the loved-one's body which were supposed to continue to rack him until he was prepared to return to the arms of his lady love. Otto Ernest Rayburn, in his *Ozark Country*, refers to a curious custom in which lovelorn maidens on May Eve suspend their handkerchiefs on bushes in the hope that on the morning after they may see in the dried dew the initials of the one they will marry. Equally fascinating is the custom in which a girl visits a spring at daybreak and there pours water into a glass in which there is an egg, in the expectation of seeing there a vision of her future husband and children. There exists also an interesting variant of the well-known Halloween mirror superstition, which in all probability relates to a period antecedent to the invention of glass, in which a girl peers into a spring of water at Halloween in the hope of seeing by the light of a burning torch the face of the man she will one day marry.

Even boys have been known to indulge in what can only be described as a kind of modernised love magic which involves muttering an incantation over a packet of chewing gum which is then offered to a girl who, if she accepts it, becomes the unresisting prisoner of love. Finally it is a sign and portent of burning interest to the boy friend that should a woman's second toe be longer than her big one she will be master in the house, or if one dares to use an Old-World allegory, the husband can expect to be under his wife's thumb.

Among the superstitions once observed by married couples was the belief that cow-peas thrown on to the road ensured fertility, while a holed stone suspended over the bed relieved the pains of a woman in labour. In the Old World the latter was known as a hagstone and was employed as an antidote to nightmares.

Superstitious folk medicines of various kinds are not yet quite obsolete and the swamp people, who are apparently extremely intelligent and resourceful, continue to draw upon local products for their needs. Powdered snake root is prescribed for headaches and corn meal for styes, while boxwood juice cures nosebleed. A type of miracle-curer known as a "snake woman" at one time administered charms and potions, performing a similar function to that of the white witch of European folklore and the Indian medicine man. Many of these specialists display distinct traces of European superstitious concepts, as in the case of the seventh son of a seventh son who not only has the power to cure warts but is very often a blood charmer.

When all else fails and the spirit of death triumphs over helpless mankind, the Ozark people fall back upon the traditional superstitions that have been handed down to them from the remote past. In common with other death superstitions the world over, the cry of a bird, in this case the whippoorwill, is a fatal omen, and likewise the hoot of an owl. It is a fairly common Ozark belief and one that may be found in a number of other communities, that a hoe or axe carried into the house brings about death in the family. This has obvious connections with the Scottish superstition that carrying a spade through the front door is a death omen and is almost certainly based upon the association of any earth-removing implement with grave-digging.

Marguerite Lyon, in her *Marge of Sunrise Mountain Farm*, refers to another interesting Ozark death omen : When the house dog falls asleep "with his paws all drawn up", he indicates by the way his tail points at the time, the direction from which the fatal news is to be expected. Like their cousins in the Old World, the Ozark people continue to perceive omens in the sky, in the odd movements of the domestic cat and dog, and in farm animals. They detect danger if a red-haired girl crosses their path on a white horse, and tremble at that infinitely greater menace—the sound of a woman whistling. Spittle and crossing fingers are commonplace antidotes to misfortune.

A great deal of study has been undertaken into the magical beliefs of these people, much of whose lore includes elements of witchcraft, for in what other light can one regard the methods of the Ozark horse-breaker who persuades his mare to give birth to a colt of a particular colour by holding a cloth of the desired colour before its eyes? As for malefic witchcraft, the witch can always be effectively disposed of by drawing her outline on a piece of wood which is then shot at with a silver bullet. In the Ozarks, a witch could be of either sex.

The researcher occasionally discovers gems of out-moded folklore which would be amusing but for the appalling social situations they seem to indicate. The author is indebted to Dr. Raymond Brown and his mother, Mrs. Brown, of Gloucester, Virginia, U.S.A., for the following intriguing examples of local lore, much of it, as might be expected, of a medical character :

A pickle placed in the mouth of a newborn baby prevents it from having colic. A newborn baby should be dressed by the feet and arms first; never the head, as this brings bad luck. In a case of nose-bleeding the cat's tail should be poked up the bleeding nostril. Another folk remedy for nosebleed is to place a small wad of newspaper beneath the upper lip. Instead of newspaper, the Negroes of Gloucester generally use cobwebs or soot. A tradition indicating distinct traces of native American origin is the attempt to cure asthma by agitating a chihuahua dog into a state of violent rage at which time (to quote) "during his anger he will then swallow the asthma". This in terms of primitive magic represents the transference of the illness to an animal, a somewhat startling discovery in twentieth-century America.

The Pennsylvania Dutch are really quite out of place in modern America, if only for the fact that their domestic harmony and piety are qualities which ought long ago to have been extinguished in a society where the guiding rule is mammon. Living to a considerable extent in the past, these modern descendants of German, Swiss and French Huguenot religious zealots retain many old-time virtues that are quite incongruous in a world where moral conventions have become overwhelmed by a permanent revolution. Spurning wealth, they dedicate their lives to God, this in itself being a truly radical departure from contemporary mores. Interwoven with their secular and religious practices are many curious superstitions inherited from their European forebears.

Among the Pennsylvania Dutch those furthest removed from the modern scene are the Old Order Amish who not only reject automobiles but even hooks and eyes on clothing since these are regarded as appendages "for Satan to hang things on". The Amish are easily recognisable by the broad-brimmed hats worn by the men and the bonnets of the women. The men are invariably bearded. They have been credited with many outlandish beliefs and despite the fact that much of this has been exaggerated, their superstitions undoubtedly provide a useful field for study if only because of their historical interest. One of the oddest of these declares that if a child's baptismal water is preserved and given him in later life he is destined to become a first-class singer. Coming events cast their shadows before in the superstition that a child who is unlucky enough to be born in a thunderstorm is doomed to die by lightning, and that an old diaper put on a child at birth foredooms him to becoming a thief. Great care must be exercised when walking near a baby, for should he be inadvertently stepped over his growth will be stunted. When first nursed the baby must be carried on the left side, or he will become left-handed, while if he is weaned in early spring he is in grave danger of becoming permanently grey-haired. Furthermore, a baby must never be tickled under the chin since this gives him a stammer. It is little wonder, therefore, that one often finds horseshoes nailed to the crib for luck, but always convex side up so that the luck will not "run out".

The elaborate precautions taken by the Amish against psychic attack leave one with the impression that the protective power of religious faith is perhaps not always quite as effective among them as one has been led to believe. It is very obvious that among certain fundamentalists religious beliefs and superstition have a complementary function, the one reinforcing the other, and that they can therefore exist quite happily side by side.

The Amish are a healthy people, perhaps because their medicine is of the folk variety and because also orthodox physicians play very little part in their lives. Cow dung is used to clear up inflammations, and rheumatism is kept successfully at bay by wearing the eye-tooth of a pig as a talisman, or by carrying a coffin nail in the pocket—a relic of seventeenth-century magical practice. Yet another curious survival, based on the old-time European faith in the healing power of the dead, is the superstition that one can cure a tumour by stroking it with the hand of a corpse. In those cases where preventive magic fails there exists a special system of treatment for the sick. Bed-sores can be avoided by laying an axe under the bed, and kidney disorders cured by regular doses of goat urine. Even an epileptic patient can be restored to health if he swallows the heart of a rattlesnake, which incidentally was an ancient American Indian god of fruitfulness and also a symbol of life.

Although the statement has been often disputed, it is a fact that many Pennsylvania Dutch have an intense fear of witchcraft. Until a generation or so ago (and perhaps even to this day) there existed a local variant of the witch doctor called the "Pow Wow Man" or "Hex Master", whose function it was to "point out" the witch, with the unhappy result that many scapegoats were brutally murdered by their neighbours. Hex signs, incidentally, are still placed on barn doors to keep evil spirits at bay, the word "hex" being based upon the name of the witch goddess "Hecate".

Even today when malefic witchcraft tends to be on the decline, magically endowed Amishmen are occasionally hired by other communities for the purpose of water-divining, which they achieve by means of a gold coin suspended in a drinking glass, following the formula : "The number of times the coin swings against the side of the glass denotes the number of feet beneath the earth the stream is located."

Perhaps it is only in those isolated communities where the original stock has avoided too close an intermingling with other types that the older forms of superstition can be found today, but even here social change threatens their extinction before the century ends. Generally speaking the lore will be found in its original state only in isolated racial or rural pockets or among deprived social groups where there exists relatively little access to fresh ideas or to the concepts of other cultures. In western Wisconsin a number of interesting superstitions have recently been brought to light of which the following are representative :

If the cat washes itself in the doorway it means that a clergyman is due to visit the house. If potatoes boil dry it is a sign of rain; while a rooster crowing before midnight indicates a change in the weather. One must never use firewood cut from a tree that has been struck by lightning as this exposes the house to similar attack. Finally there is an interesting fishing superstition :

> Fish East means fish bite least,
> Fish West, fish bite best.

Among the racially or socially depressed in the American scene superstition retains a very strong hold, largely for the reason that the poverty-stricken are always among the most conservative in any community, their imaginations rarely soaring beyond the vista of a living wage. The poorer whites and the Negroes of Louisiana have a lore which displays Indian, Spanish and Anglo-Saxon influences, but the superstitions themselves are based upon well-established magical principles to be found all over the world. To cure a wart one steals a piece of meat which is then rubbed upon the wart and buried in the ground, and as the meat rots, so does the wart. In a Louisianan variant of the same superstition the site for the burial must be where rain can drip upon it from the house gutters. A method of transferring a wart from an animal to a tree was described by Hilda Roberts in her book *Creole*, published some forty years ago : "To cure a wart on a horse lead him up to a pecan tree, touch the wart with a nail, and scratch a cross on the tree with the nail. As soon as the cross grows up the wart disappears."

Spittle has long been regarded as a prophylactic agent with healing and magical powers. It dispels black magic, evil-wishing and sickness and is a creative force. In certain mythologies the gods created the first life from spittle, which is why it continues to symbolise purgation and purification. Among the poor of Louisiana spittle superstitions are apparently obsessional. They will spit if they see a caterpillar or a cross-eyed person, or when they are bitten by an insect. They spit when they lose anything and they spit upon a finger if a foot goes to sleep. Sneezing is, if anything, even more significant than spitting since, like the shudder, it is one of those involuntary acts which have always been regarded as indicative of some supernatural presence, more often a sign that an evil spirit is attempting to enter the body via the nose. In Louisiana, as in the British Isles, it is axiomatic that the sneeze indicates what the fates hold in store for the superstitiously minded.

> Sneeze on Monday, sneeze for danger.
> Sneeze on Tuesday, kiss a stranger.
> Sneeze on Wednesday, sneeze for a letter.
> Sneeze on Thursday, something better.
> Sneeze on Friday, sneeze for sorrow.
> Sneeze on Saturday, see your beau (in England : true love) tomorrow.
> Sneeze on Sunday, the Devil will have you the rest of the week.

It is a lamentable fact that in Louisiana a sneeze can have still more depressing implications, for to sneeze when thirteen people are sitting at table means that either the oldest or the youngest present will die within a twelvemonth. It also appears that if you sneeze at table you can expect a companion to share the next meal. Finally, should someone sneeze when a statement is made, it is an infallible sign from the spirits that the truth has been told.

The people of Louisiana have preserved a number of interesting superstitions relating to childhood. If the first journey of a newborn baby is upstairs then it will become high-minded in later life, but on the other hand if the over-enthusiastic parent tosses his child into the air it is likely to become a dimwit. In the age of the academic rat-race it must be of the greatest comfort to Louisiana parents with ambitions for their child's future to be told that a bald-headed baby is destined to become a brilliant scholar. A child's destiny can also be determined by placing a Bible, a silver dollar and a pack of playing cards within arm's reach. If it seizes the cards first it will be a gambler, if the dollar a financier, but if it grabs the Bible its future is assured in both this world and the next, as it is destined to become a preacher. Among other intriguing survivals is the custom of placing sulphur (the fumes of the Devil) in a child's shoes to prevent influenza, or blowing tobacco smoke on to its stomach as an insurance against colic.

The Negroes of the United States, particularly in the old south, have retained much of their distinct cultural identity despite the intermingling of their African mythology with that of the European. Authentic African myths persist in not dissimilar form to that in which they were first introduced from Africa two to three hundred years ago. Legends associated with the old gods of Africa may still be found in the United States and in the West Indies and Brazil. The surviving elements of the older magical beliefs have been reduced in the main to superstitions of a more general character which combine elements of both African and European culture. Rural Negroes are still fearful of the ignis fatuus, or will-o'-the-wisp, which has the unpleasant habit of luring its victims to their deaths in rivers or streams and which utters the hideous cry, "Aie, aie, mo gagnin toi. Ai, Ai, I have you".

There is a very close parallel between some of the contemporary American Negro superstitions and the more familiar European type. To turn back on a journey is ominous, and to offset any resultant disaster it becomes necessary to "make a cross mark on the ground and pull a strand of hair from the head and throw it in the direction in which you intend to travel". The marking of a cross as a protective ritual act is very common among Southern Negroes, and is done whenever a rabbit is met on the road, in which case the traveller also takes three steps backwards, turns to the right and spits. Marking a cross is not merely the antidote for bad luck but in the past at least was a device for the exorcism of physical pains that were supposedly due to witchcraft. A similar ritual is followed when a stranger is met while on a journey, presumably on the offchance that he could be the Devil.

There is an interesting parallel between the lore of white and black in the old slave superstition which held that to sweep dust from the doorstep at night meant that the sweeper would have the misfortune to be sold in the slave market, which is closely allied to the European belief that sweeping dust out of the house sweeps away the household luck. This type of broomstick superstition crops up time and time again among peoples all over the world. There is apparently more than a coincidence in the fact that the witch is so closely associated with the magic broom.

Among amulets favoured by American Negroes are silver rings inscribed with Chinese characters, or rings of iron manufactured from horseshoe nails. The most powerful type of protective magic, however, is provided by the familiar rabbit's foot charm.

That apparently permanently submerged element in American society, the Indian, has a special contribution to make in the way of superstitious lore. There has always existed among the Indians a vast body of tradition handed down from the remote past, comprising songs, legends, proverbs and riddles, and ritual prayers which continue to play some part in tribal life today although the oral lore is in grave danger of dying out with the passing of the older members of the tribes. The Apaches use certain ritual words which are supposed to have the power to keep evil spirits at bay and to afford protection against disease; in every case the efficacy of a charm is dependent upon its secrecy. Amulets were once an essential ingredient of Indian protective magic and took some unusual forms. The Apaches warded off illness with buckskin bags filled with pollen, and the Hopi Indians constructed amulets from petrified wood, while the Iroquois manufactured miniature canoes which they believed supplied protection against the risk of death from drowning.

Wherever there is love there will be found love magic, and among North American Indians this often takes the form of special songs or charms known as love medicines, for which the Cree Indians were once famous. Indian love magic seems to have found favour among the ordinary citizens of the U.S.A. for Navajo squaws have ruthlessly exploited the current revival in magical beliefs by the commercialisation of love beads, each of which is supposedly filled with powerful Indian magic but which usually prove to be necklaces of berries strung upon nylon thread. The squaws, who are normally on public relief, can at last make a good living by trafficking upon the superstitious beliefs of the so-called civilised whites. The Navajo Indians, ever ready to move with the times, now market an owl fetish which, immediately after manufacture, is scrutinised to ensure that only second-class magic is sold to the customer, the best being carefully retained for Indian use only. Owl fetishes are now in great demand in the United States since they offer an almost certain guarantee of success in university examinations, the owl being the symbol of wisdom.

The meeting point between the primitive superstitions of the Negro, the Indian and the Caucasian is provided by the cult of black magic, now well established in the United States. Fear of the hex is still strong and finds its most powerful expression among the Negroes who believe implicitly in the possibility of becoming "hoodooed" should a snake bone ever be placed by an enemy under one's pillow or if black pepper and salt are found sprinkled upon the front doorstep. Sometimes black magic takes the form of a hoodoo bag containing weeds and red flannel and various other, unmentionable ingredients. It is generally accepted that in order to acquire the power of a hoodoo it is first necessary to sell one's soul to the Devil. In a recent English *Daily Telegraph* Supplement article entitled "Voodoo", the full range of underground occultism in New York is brought into the light of day. Apparently there are "voodoo shops" which retail graveyard dust, bat's blood and pigeon's eyes, hate prayers, and hexing candles which are supposed to make the victim die. An individual who has been "hoodooed" usually betrays the fact from the sudden appearance of peculiar marks on his body. White magic, expressly devised to counteract the black variety, is also available in the form of an "All-purpose jinx chasing spray". There exists also a flourishing trade in phials of "dragon's blood" for use by neglected virgins, together with a vast array of magical herbs, and lucky charms, not to mention a "money drawing incense to be burned at midnight while thinking aloud about rolls of dollar bills".

Perhaps the most remarkable of all the currently held superstitious beliefs of American life is the supposed power of the evil eye, which threatens any child who is inadvertently praised. Cure can be effected, however, by the power of spittle. It is particularly strong among those of Italian stock and is known also to the Indians. Under its old name—overlooking—it even lingers on as a superstition among those of Anglo-Saxon ancestry.

Possibly the most interesting and unexpected demonstration of the way in which basic patterns of superstitious beliefs may be reasserted and even transformed by situations involving stress was provided by an investigation carried out among 25,000 interned Japanese

Americans at Tule Lake, California, during the Second World War, these unhappy people having apparently become reconciled to the worst. Almost overnight the impact of war and the overriding influence of fear led paradoxically to the rejection of most of their luck-bringing amulets, and in their place gloomy prognostication and the dark omens of hopelessness reigned supreme. Some of the latter were of the universal pattern, i.e. "If you point at a funeral line you will be the first to die" or "If three persons are photographed together the middle one will die first". Others were no doubt traditional to the Japanese way of life, examples being "If you feel sorry for a sick animal you will become ill; when it dies you too will die". "Don't sleep with your head pointing north (the Buddhist burial ground) or death will follow." And finally and perhaps most melancholy of all : "If a cat jumps over a corpse that has been laid out for burial the dead person will be transformed into a vampire."

CHAPTER XII

THE LORE OF MANY LANDS

THE ULTIMATE sources of the world's superstitions may never be known for they belong to pre-history, those vast unrecorded epochs of time during which customs and language evolved, became transformed and finally settled into the mould in which they exist today. The continuous migrations of peoples, and the amalgamations of communities during this period have modified the early social units beyond recognition, but the basic structure of belief has remained the same, if for no other reason than that man appears to be fundamentally unchangeable.

This power of traditional lore was brought to the fore recently when the author accepted an invitation to participate in a discussion on surviving Scottish superstitions, arranged by Grampian Television on (perhaps appropriately) Friday the 13th, 1970. The day was notable for the fact that, by some remarkable coincidence, only two vessels of the Aberdeen fishing fleet had put to sea. The owners' comments can be summed up as : "It just happened that way" or "There's no sense in taking chances".

The superstitions of Scotland include a number of curious variations upon the more familiar themes and for that reason deserve to be recorded before they become modified by changes in the social life which preserved them for so long. Among Scotland's bad-luck-bringers may be found the following unexpected examples :

It is a sign of forthcoming national disaster if three swans are seen flying together, and of personal trouble ahead if a triangular crease is discovered in a sheet when making up a bed, as this symbolises a coffin. One must never wear red and green together, or stand with one's back to the edge of the door, or throw greenstuffs on to the fire. In this latter example there is perhaps an allusion to the psychic dangers consequent upon burning winter greenery. It is even more dangerous to post a love letter on Christmas Day, February 29th or September 1st. Needless to say, it is unlucky to carry a spade through the house, for a grave will soon be dug, since by this action one symbolically brings death into the home. Based on the same principle is the superstition that it is very ominous if a spade is waved to attract attention. However, one form of defence is to hurl a handful of earth in the direction of the person who commits this outrage. In the Shetlands a kind of lichen called crotal, which grows on the sea-girt rocks, is used to dye wool for Harris tweed. Local fishermen, however, will not wear crotal at sea because of the superstition, "crotal always returns to the rocks", with its implication that the wearer is doomed to drown.

The Celts of Ireland are, if anything, even more overwhelmed by superstitious lore than the Scots, refusing to build broken tombstones into the fabric of their cottages and preserving reverently the "fairy fort", the sacred tree that grows at the centre of their fields, and they have even been known to tap the tyres of a new car to drive out the evil spirits. To those who enjoy attending Irish wakes it might be helpful to know that "it is very lucky to have drink spilled over you as drink spilled on the ground is good for the fairies", this being a relic of the ancient libation in which one shared one's repast with the supernatural powers.

When browsing through the recorded lore of more distant lands one becomes aware time and time again of the common characteristics underlying all the superstitions of the world. Between Westernised man with his boasted science and the surviving primitive, however, there is a clear-cut difference in attitude, for whereas the former is somewhat shamefaced about his superstitions the latter is usually prepared to avow them quite openly. This rule is very apparent in the case of the educated classes of the emergent nations, where there exists a strong tendency to despise the cultural heritage of the superstitious peasantry.

Even the modern Maltese, for example, is often reluctant to discuss the old custom in which the churches of Malta were made to display two clock-faces, one showing the correct time and the other a false time, a device employed by superstitious churchgoers to deceive the Devil as to the time of the church service since it appears he always went soul-hunting on a Sunday. As one Maltese official told the author: "This was in the old days, of course. We don't like to talk of such things nowadays."

It is often only in dribs and drabs that one is able to extract the curious beliefs and practices of other European communities, as for example the role of the psychic healer in Normandy and Brittany. Such an individual invariably claims to be the seventh son of a seventh son, and while disclaiming any pretence to

Unlucky to spill the salt.

To restore the luck—throw a pinch of salt over the left shoulder, right into the Devil's face.

The oak tree is sacred to Thor the Thunder God—an acorn in the pocket protects you from disasters of all kinds.

magic, invariably prescribes remedies that are based purely and simply on suggestion.

In Southern and Eastern Europe the fear of the evil eye has always been strong. The Yugoslav touches his biceps to ward off its ill-effect, while the Italian rattles keys at the approach of a *jetta-tore*, as one with the power of the evil eye is known. Antidotes to the evil eye are by no means restricted to touching biceps or cold iron or rattling keys, however, and special protective gestures are made with the fingers. As a curious survival from the days of phallic worship plastic neck-charms with very obvious sexual characteristics are still worn on necklaces in Mediterranean lands, and are sometimes brought back to Northern Europe in all innocence by returning holiday-makers. In Sicily, an island with a high infant mortality rate, the local equivalent of the witch-doctor is in constant demand to charm away disaster to babies threatened by the evil eye.

A few years ago a famous magician, described as "The Wizard of Tobruk", was sentenced to two years' enforced residence in a small North Italian town as a means of restricting his influence over the lives of the Sicilians. In keeping with the highest principles of commercialised magic he had despatched what were described as "magic waves" to dupes all over Italy, and had built up a large clientele among the superstitious women of Rome. His official offence was stated to be illegally practising medicine and "predicting the future without a commercial licence". More recently, a self-styled magician of Rome charmed away the wife of one of his clients and followed it up by bewitching him into handing over his entire property, including his house.

Old superstitions lingering on in Mediterranean areas have an easily recognisable connection with pagan worship. At the approach of a storm the fisherman still pours a glass of wine into the waters, perhaps even now as a tribute to the spirits of the sea. Greek sponge fishers offset a storm by carving a cross into the mast of their ship and then sticking a knife into it. The person who carries out this rite is conscious of committing a sin however and usually offers to undergo some form of penance. The author and traveller Norman Lewis, writing of Ibiza, says: "Out of a submerged reverence for the old gods of the sea no priest was allowed to set foot in a fisherman's boat." In Scotland even today no clergyman is permitted to board the fisherman's boat, for reasons that have there been forgotten.

A miscellany of other European superstitions confirms the

uniformity of the traditional pattern. It is in Iceland, where oddly enough there was actually a time when a ghost could be legally summoned before a court of law and bound over to keep the peace, that an interesting array of superstitions, obviously of Scandinavian origin, may still be found, among the older elements in the population. As might be expected, it is the fishermen who provide the most interesting examples. There is a reluctance among many fishermen to commence work on a Monday, which is apparently the "taboo" day, as is Friday among their English and Scottish counterparts. It is unlucky to shoot at the sea-birds which follow the fishing boat. There is a hint of the Troll or elemental spirit in the Icelandic tradition of "small people living in stones" whose activities can be either capricious or harmful, like the more familiar elves of our own mythology.

Icelandic traditions are of great interest for they represent a very old strata of belief indeed. An example is the superstition that if an unmarried person sits at the corner of a table he or she will not marry for seven years, which corresponds closely to the American superstition that an unmarried woman who witnesses the laying of a cornerstone may not expect to be married for at least a year. Among the more unusual type of Icelandic lore are the following birth superstitions: A pregnant woman who steps over a cat in the mating season will give birth to a hermaphrodite, while if she eats a ptarmigan egg the child will be freckled. It is equally dangerous for her to drink from a cracked cup as the child will then have a harelip. It is obvious that the magical aspects of birth continue to be of immense significance in northern lands.

The superstitions of the Dutch have a good deal in common with those of the British, and equally familiar is the reluctance of the average Dutch citizen to admit to them. When knocking on wood for luck the Dutchman considers it necessary to touch the base or unpainted underside of the table. Like many English and American gamblers, a loser at the gaming tables will place his handkerchief on the seat of his chair. Teddy bear mascots are apparently as fashionable among Dutch goalkeepers as they are with the English yachtsman, and there are several local variations of motor-car superstition, although the myth that washing a car automatically brings down the rain is not generally known in Holland. Magical aids for safety on the road are plentiful enough, one of the more popular mascots being the photograph of a sweetheart attached to the dashboard.

Hostility to red hair is still fairly strong in Holland as it is in all those other lands once invaded by the Danes, and those with red hair are in consequence regarded as agents of misfortune.

In Denmark most of the better-known superstitions may be found, albeit with local variations. To break a looking glass in Zealand brings either seven years' good luck or seven years' bad luck, dependent upon how the fates happen to be disposed at the time but with an emphasis upon the unlucky aspect. There exists also a localised version of the salt-spilling superstition. To upset dry salt brings good luck but if it is wet the luck will be bad. It is proverbial in Denmark, however, that salt is nearly always damp because of the climate. Danish children bring their lucky charms into the examination room but in the main these are to attract good luck rather than avert failure. Many Danes maintain luck on the road by suspending mascots beneath their car mirrors. Fox tails attached to motorbikes represent a revival of latter-day totemism among the younger generation.

Greenland, an outpost of Danish civilisation, can offer as ritual objects grotesque Eskimo charms made from whale or walrus bone, and sometimes little amulets in the shape of fish. Other Eskimos scatter on the ground the feathers of the ptarmigan they shoot, believing that this ensures a plentiful supply of these birds.

Of all the countries of modern Europe that remain deeply steeped in occult doctrines, the most strongly affected of course is Germany. The fanatical German witch-hunters of the sixteenth and seventeenth centuries and the Jew-baiters of the twentieth belonged to a nation that has perhaps never been wholly Christianised, and this provides a possible explanation for some of their magical practices. The personalisation of evil in the form of a helpless minority is a familiar device of power-seekers who can thereby trade upon the deeply entrenched anxieties of the masses by exploiting their superstitious fears. Convince the people that the Jew has placed his curse upon the nation and the Jew-baiter, like the witch-doctor, can demand power as the price of taking off the spell. The "Devil Jew" has served as a convenient victim for oppressors of all kinds during the past 2,000 years and will no doubt do so again. Is there, one wonders, an element of a troubled conscience in the superstition that even today no birds will ever sing at Dachau? The powerful emphasis that the Germans place upon blood, soil and race, all of which are based upon tribal superstitions, provides the mystique and the dynamic upon which neo-paganism thrives. Even with the decline of the Nazi system the old spirit continues to be manifested in some of the superstitions of modern Germany. Paul Bauer has revealed in his *Christianity or Superstition* the strength of the current belief in German black witchcraft which has resulted in the cruel persecution of innocent old women. In one such case a woman was denounced by her neighbours for drawing black crosses on their doorsteps to bring trouble upon their homes as a result of which cows had fallen sick and hens had stopped laying. In Germany today the divining rod and the pendulum have become common-place and, "Amulets and talismen for warding off misfortune are manufactured in great quantities; quacks extol their wonder drugs which they have obtained from abroad; exorcists offer powerful protection against witches and evil spirits".

Almost all of our surviving superstitions represent variations upon age-old principles. In Central Europe a severe storm indicates that someone has hanged himself, whereas in old-time England it meant that a wizard was about to be admitted to Hell. European Russians are so obsessed by the magical virtues of water that the Soviet government was compelled some years ago to take forcible action to prevent a newly-constructed reservoir from being used as a reposi-tory for coins dropped into it by peasants who desired only to pay tribute to the water spirits. In Hungary the lovelorn girl turns to magic clothing to get her man, choosing the most effective device she knows—the polka-dot dress.

The European Jew has preserved a number of interesting super-stitions, most of which belong to his Middle Eastern homeland, though others have been absorbed into his culture during the centuries he has wandered like a pariah through the countries of Europe. The Jews as a whole are an extremely superstitious people whose folklore has become integrated with their religion. This is apparent in the very strongly imputed moral prohibition against a pregnant woman visiting a cinema showing a horror film, or a zoo, or even approaching a known enemy, in case harm should befall her unborn child. If she is frightened by any animal or insect the Jewess must never touch her face in case her baby "should be marked in any way". Should anyone say to a child, "How beautiful you are" or pass any compliment, the influence of the evil eye is threatened but it can always be offset by chanting to the child three times in Yiddish, "Whoever gave you the evil eye may it fall on them". A child must never be watched while it sleeps because of the close similarity between this action and the custom of watching the dead, nor must it be shown its reflection until it has grown its first tooth, which corresponds to the Anglo-Saxon belief that a child must not look into a mirror until it has attained its first year.

The supposed power of the voice to translate fears into hideous realities lies behind the Jewish superstition that if one person discusses with another the misfortunes of an absent third party there is a danger of their suffering a similar fate. It is possible to protect oneself against this calamity but only if the first person says immediately to the other "It shouldn't happen to you". One must be extremely cautious when discussing another's boil never to touch one's own face as this transfers the blemish to oneself.

At the Jewish funeral no animal is allowed near the coffin because of the fear that the departing soul will try to enter its body, a superstition having affinities with the Japanese belief that the animal becomes a vampire. If anyone sneezes while a dead person is under discussion it is necessary to pull one's ears by the lobes and say at the same time : "They in their world, we in ours." Among the more general Jewish superstitions are the following :

To spill salt means a fight. The sight of a black cat is an omen of death. A piece of "twig" of an unusual shape floating in a teacup means that a letter is on its way.

Those other hopeless wanderers upon the face of the earth, the gipsies, have accumulated a large body of superstitions in their journeyings, some of which can probably be traced to the Romanies' original home, India. No gipsy likes to eat food that has been stepped over, nor will he drink from a stream over which a woman has walked. Among German gipsies a caravan that has been used for a confinement is considered defiled and must be burned, as are all caravans after the deaths of their owners.

The lore of the East incorporates many superstitions which bear a close affinity to those of the West. The Oriental, however, has not merely the evil eye to contend with but the evil mouth and the evil voice. Talismen and amulets provide commonplace forms of defence and even the Moslem protects himself against evil with a bird symbol, which is not regarded as unclean, accompanied by a sentence from the Koran or a prayer. In India, as in Europe, one offsets the power of evil by burying an iron object beneath the doorway.

The Chinese are subject to superstitious fears that represent an intermingling of legend and protective magic. A powerful symbol in Chinese lore is the weasel, which has an uncanny influence over those who are sick or near death and which is supposed to have the power to take possession of any individual whom it comes upon unawares. Its victim utters a kind of gibberish which gradually begins to take the form of oracular utterances. In order to expel the weasel from its human abode it is necessary to obey the animal's wishes as revealed through the mouth of its victim, for only then will the diabolical animal agree to leave its habitation. Understandably, perhaps, the weasel is regarded by the Chinese with considerable awe and never killed. Equally sacrosanct is the fox, whose habitat can only be disturbed at the risk of some disaster falling upon the head of the offender. It is said that a man who digs up a fox's burrow may expect to become demented, and it is not unknown for the den to be protected and food to be placed at its entrance.

The fear of the unquiet dead is far stronger in China than in Europe, for a suicide can be expected to haunt the site of his death almost indefinitely. This is poignantly illustrated by a story told to the author which described how "a man in grief at the deaths of his parents chained himself to an elm growing near their graves and died of voluntary starvation. When the Japanese subsequently tried to build a road they attempted to cut down the tree but four people died in doing so." The road was finally re-routed away from the site.

The symbolic number seven crops up in the Chinese superstition that a ghost returns to its old home on the seventh night following death. Among other Chinese death superstitions are the following reminders of the ghoulish bonds that unite all mankind since they are all based on universal themes. Any death by accident, murder or foul play is to be feared since the ghost may be expected to return and seek revenge. Among omens a hooting owl near the house is a sign of forthcoming family disaster, usually death or illness. And finally, and perhaps requiring no comment, if a bird's droppings fall upon you it is to be regarded as an omen of misfortune.

The ever-recurring theme of the broom symbol and the ritual act of sweeping is found in the Chinese superstition that by sweeping one expels all good fortune from the home. If the floor is swept or anything ill said of another person between December 31st and January 5th then bad luck befalls the whole family.

The Chinese use peach stones as amulets, whereas the Japanese rely upon the psychic properties of fruit and flowers to protect their homes against the forces of evil, or they hang garlic, the healing plant, above their doors as a first line of defence against the attacks of disease. Japanese omens display the same underlying principles as the European variety. A comb picked up with teeth facing the body

is as unlucky in Japan as is a knife so picked up in the west. To kill a
spider in the morning destroys the spirit of the human soul that has
entered its body while in a state of sleep. In Europe we say "If you
wish to live and thrive, let a spider run alive". Most cats bring bad
luck, with the honourable exception of the three-coloured variety,
which is supposed to be a luck-bringer. The Japanese have a strong
prejudice against eating a certain crab, whose shell closely resembles
the face of the Heike warriors who drowned themselves in medieval
times after being defeated in battle.

To enter a domain where the power of magic has always flour-
ished with undiminished vigour it is necessary to turn to the African
continent, where superstition competes successfully with science for
control of the African mind. The imposition and removal of curses
has always been one of the more disreputable aspects of the magical
arts, and in Africa one comes upon some remarkable manifestations
of this. Fear of the evil eye is very common in North Africa where
blue beads are worn as a form of defence against this type of psychic
attack. Egypt appears to be almost as obsessed with magic as in the
days of the Pharaohs, particularly when one examines the lore of the
peasantry. A recent survey into the psychiatric state of Egyptians
finds hysterical symptoms to be "perhaps the commonest neurotic
manifestations in Europe", these being "attributed to witchcraft
spirits and the evil eye". Those afflicted are placed in the care of
native healers and certain traditional cults. A study of comparative
psychiatry in the Northern Sudan repeats the same story. "Hysteria
is predominantly a female disorder as mania is in males—auditory
hallucinations are attributed to Satan. As one would expect the
treatment of schizophrenia lies in the hands of fakirs and native
healers."

Black Africa is almost entirely dominated by magic. In the
article, "The Magical Roots of African Political Power" (*New
Society*, Jan. 9th, 1969) occurs the statement: "In the majority of
African societies power of the most basic kind belongs to those who
know how to manipulate certain symbolic objects, divinatory
counters and 'medicines'." The doctors of magic are divided into
two distinct classes, firstly the diviner who identifies the evil agency
and secondly the healer who drives it from the body of the
sufferer. Fear of witchcraft is the mainspring of the witch-doctor's
power. In some societies spirit mediumship is practised, notably by
"the Ashanti of Ghana and the Shona of Rhodesia".

Great political influence can be acquired by magicians who banish evil ghosts, cure the possessed and remove curses. A witch-doctor can extend his influence even to the expatriate African abroad. To the author's own knowledge there are Africans living in London who are still paying the witch-doctor back home "protection money" to ward off evil spirits.

The exploitation of superstitious fears and human gullibility has been developed to a fine art among Africans and there must be many a European psycho-fakir who envies his witch-doctor counterpart his ability to extort money from his dupes. Some years ago an African bank cashier was persuaded to hand over the entire contents of his till to a fakir disguised as a mermaid.

Witchcraft continues to be so powerful a factor in African life that in Ghana it has actually been outlawed. Many Ghanaians accept without question the existence of flying witches, and shrines have been actually set up to protect the community from their attacks, while even trial by ordeal is sometimes imposed to discover the witch's identity. Among the many magical aids employed to counteract dangerous spells is vaccination by means of a black powder injected into the body which is supposed to make the blood so bitter that no witch cares to taste it. Magical charms are employed by Africans to secure protection against witches, and magic rings, pots and stones are dispensed to the community by the priests of the anti-witchcraft shrines. More recently foreign charms and talismen have been imported into African countries in large quantities and a rapidly developing mail-order industry has succeeded in popularising a vast array of American-manufactured charms which are regarded as part of the white man's magic and are therefore considered to be the source of his economic power. Sometimes even paper money and most certainly the cheque, is assumed to have magical properties, for how otherwise could an ordinary piece of paper covered with printed symbols acquire the power to conjure up goods and services out of thin air?

If the European is dominant socially it is assumed that he has access to some superior type of magic, and with this in mind the newly-educated African studies *Napoleon's Book of Fate,* or purchases a photograph of Charles Atlas, the muscle man, to be used as a "strength fetish". Charms of this type, it must be pointed out, are utilised for both defence and attack.

The advance of Westernised forms of culture seems to have had little effect upon the basic superstitious attitudes of the African whether in peace or war. In the battles of the Congo and in the more recent civil war in Nigeria, the witch-doctor immunised the warriors against hostile bullets with magical rites and it has been even suggested that in the Biafran defeat magic played as important a role as weapons of war. Superstition survives every type of social change and the witch-doctor now moves into more sophisticated surroundings to apply his magic to the emotional problems of the university student. In southern Africa some of the awe of black man's magic has rubbed off on to the Europeans, who will often admit to a sneaking belief in the powers of African occultism. At the same time, because of the need by the ruling race to preserve the myth of a basic difference between black and white, the European has created a demonology in which the black man is equated with either gross ignorance or unmitigated evil and is to be kept at bay if not with white magic then with white man's magic, powder and shot.

Included in the prevailing mythology of the South African whites, for instance, there is a generally accepted myth which justifies the repressive measures imposed by the state with the argument that the only alternative is armed revolt, rape and chaos. There is a deep and complex problem here for, on the one hand, the African is credited with supernatural powers, while at the same time it is maintained that he can be held in submission by purely physical means.

Some of the most interesting individual superstitions of black Africa are observed by the Yorubas and Elfik tribes of Nigeria, not only because they are representative of African beliefs as a whole but because of their close similarity to the more familiar superstitions of Europe. Among these are found the following interesting beliefs about birth: The last child to be born is the one most likely to have clairvoyant powers (in Europe it is the seventh child—and preferably the seventh child of a seventh child). Should the first child conceived by the wife die, the next daughter who lives is destined to lose her own first child. It is an unlucky omen for a woman to deliver twins and because of this superstition the parents are segregated from village life. If a child is stillborn it is a clear indication that one or other of the parents has been evil. Incidentally, death by accident, murder or foul play is regarded as evidence of some evil committed by the deceased, a relic of the ancient belief that there can be no such thing as natural death.

Closely allied to European symbolism is the belief that a shooting star portends that someone is going to die. If a mouse be seen about the house it means that a ghost is near, and to banish it either incense or a candle must be burned. (In European mythology the mouse is the symbol of the soul.) Animals play an immense role in the superstitions of the Elfik people. If a cow delivers twins, both calves and cow must be destroyed or bad luck will befall the entire family. A black cat venturing inside the house means bad luck and must be chased away and the floor swept clean. A white, yellow or multicoloured cat is a good luck-bringer.

Birds, both diurnal and nocturnal, are the focal point of many Nigerian superstitions. "If a crow caws near a house it means that someone in that area will die", a superstition that is apparently as much indigenous to Africa as Europe. The sparrow and the guinea fowl are birds of good omen, and if they nest in the garden anything that is touched becomes a "money spinner". Considering that the vulture lives upon offal, it is not surprising to discover that its droppings bring lifelong poverty to the luckless person upon whom they happen to fall. An owl that hoots near the house is the metamorphosis of a witch, and if a tarantula spider "thumps up and down under the bed" it is a clear warning that the witch is approaching.

The African like the European has his ladder superstition, for a pregnant woman who walks under a ladder may expect a difficult birth. The sneezing European says, "Bless you", but the more generous African wishes you, "Health, wealth, prosperity and children".

Finally one turns to a superstitious theme that recurs in every type of culture—that of the broom and sweeping. In Nigeria it is believed that to sweep a house during the night brings bad luck; on the other hand all evil things should be expelled from the house by a thorough-going sweeping first thing in the morning. The worst thing that you can do is to strike a person with a broom; if a male is hit he becomes impotent unless he retaliates with seven blows delivered with the same broom, but a woman who is struck will be unable to keep her man and for this there exists no magical remedy. To sweep after a person as he leaves the house rids the home of all bad spirits.

Everywhere in Africa the ghosts are greatly feared on the basis that "all ghosts are evil", but whereas in Europe an occult presence is indicated by a shivering sensation ("someone is walking over my grave") the Yorubra tribesman says "If while walking alone in the afternoon or night your head feels either very light or heavy this means that there is a ghost around. The only way to save yourself is to carry something that gives off a powerful odour. This terrifies the ghost."

The common bond uniting all humanity is clearly observable in these superstitious beliefs of many lands. There are differences of a fundamental character between the peoples of the five continents it is true, but when confronted by forces that are apparently beyond control they turn as one to the ancient religion of magic, and to the superstitious rites handed down from the infancy of the human race.

CHAPTER XIII

SUPERSTITIONS AND THE GREAT

There is a tide in the affairs of men,
Which, taken at the flood, leads on to fortune

SAYS THE Bard, repeating an age-old superstition shared by all humanity that human affairs move in cycles or, to keep to the spirit of the quotation, display a tidal ebb and flow. So deeply embedded is superstition in the human psyche that one is inclined to speculate upon the role that it has played in the history of men and nations.

Of one thing we may be certain : most of the great strategists and constructive thinkers of the past were often deeply superstitious men, obsessed not only with a Messianic sense of mission but also devotees of those minor paganisms, the lucky charm, the belief in lucky and unlucky days, together with those highly personalised systems of omens and auguries by which they sought to regulate not only their personal lives but also—incredible as it may seem—affairs of state.

Undoubtedly the first lesson of social progress was the discovery that magic simply did not work, and it is somewhat surprising, therefore, to find that so many of the grandiose plans of the world's leaders came to successful fruition, and that monarchs or generals, clutching amulets or muttering incantations to the gods of victory, were able for a brief hour at least to reshape the destinies of mankind. On the other hand it ought to be taken into account that all human beings, whatever their degree, are attracted towards the supernatural in times of crisis, and that therefore the magic charm, by shielding the adventurer or the soldier from the inhibiting effect of the devils of doubt, might well have contributed to the state of mind necessary for the achievement of victory.

The culture of the ancient civilisations was dominated by superstition and by its agents, the seers and magicians. Egypt was both the mother of superstition and of science, a curious world

where faith and reason walked hand in hand, where every object
had its reflection or soul.

The Greeks were not a notoriously superstitious people, yet even
the great Socrates could be as hesitant at the prospect of challeng-
ing the gods by presuming upon fate as any unlettered peasant or
slave. "Let us not boast," he said, "lest some evil eye should put to
flight the word which I am about to speak." Alexander the Great,
conqueror of the East, was another slave of superstition; he
became so depressed by the predictions of the Chaldean priests
that his entry into Babylon would be fatal to him that he sought
refuge from his inner doubts in a series of debauches which led to
that very fever which brought about his death at the early age of
thirty-three.

The Romans, masters of the ancient world, allowed themselves
to be tricked by their seers, who claimed to read from the entrails
of sacrificed animals portents of the future, and so superstitious
were they that they would defer commencing any venture, or even
taking a meal, until assured that the gods were favourable to the
enterprise. For a Roman even to take a haircut was quite an
adventure, since it was supposed to cause a thunderstorm. The
Rome of the Caesars swarmed with soothsayers, fortune-tellers and
sellers of love philtres, most of which, if not actually lethal, were
utterly useless. For the peace of mind of the legionary it was
necessary, when returning from conquest, to be ritually purified
from the stigma of bloodshed by passing under a triumphal arch.
Julius Caesar, as is well known, was as awed as any private soldier
by the signs of the supernatural. One tends to think of these
world-shaking men of history as confident voyagers borne by an
irresistible tide of destiny towards a single goal which never left
their thoughts or dreams. Yet what do we find on that fatal night
in 44 B.C. when Caesar's sleep was disturbed by threatening
nightmares? At this time the Senate was prepared to honour
Caesar with the title of King but their messenger, recognising the
cause of his hesitancy, said to him: "If you are persuaded this is
your unlucky day you must go and tell them yourself that the
business should be put off for another time." Before Caesar's death,
so Suetonius tells us, an ominous fear hung over Rome like a
cloud. Calpurnia, Caesar's wife, was overwhelmed by the gravest
of apprehensions as the hour of fate approached.

Mahomet, whose violent religious revolution swept into oblivion
the older superstitious usages of the Arab peoples, triumphed not

by faith and force of arms alone, but to a considerable degree as the result of the superstitious qualities vested in him by his followers, who were perfectly ready to accept that even trees went forth to meet him and that he had the power to raise the dead. There is also a tradition that Mahomet had between his shoulders a curious mark which was regarded by the Arabs as a symbol of destiny. Mahomet no doubt deferred to the universal rule of history that if one intends to ride to power on the backs of a superstitious multitude one must outshine the superstitious marvels of one's predecessors.

The great comet of 1066 was supposed by the English to provide an omen of coming disaster, which seemed to be fulfilled by the Norman invasion of that year. At nine in the morning of the day of the landing on the Sussex coast of England near Beachy Head Duke William leapt ashore from his ship the *Mora*, stumbled and fell and his nose began to bleed. The act of stumbling has always been seen as an omen of misfortune and it seems possible that, if William had not possessed the presence of mind to shout : "By the splendour of God I have taken seisen of England" (seisen being a token of possession in the transfer of land), his followers might well have faltered and the battle have been lost before it had even begun.

There is even the possibility that Christopher Columbus might never have completed his voyage to America if he had given way to the superstitious apprehensions of his men, who regarded the large number of sharks that followed the ship as portents of coming disaster. Yet Columbus, once he had made his landing in the New World, could be as superstitious as the rest, for he attributed all the delays and disasters he encountered to the witchcraft of the Indians.

A little later in history, Frobisher, voyaging among the ice and snow of North America, found his efforts frustrated by the time-wasting treasure-seeking of his seamen, who took for granted that the large number of spiders they met with provided an infallible sign from the gods that gold was buried there.

The role played by superstition as an influence on the course of history is astounding. King Henry VIII, for example, is said to have become persuaded that he had been trapped into falling in love with Anne Boleyn by witchcraft. The extent to which the ages of faith and the leaders of Christendom subscribed to superstitions of obvious pagan implications was truly amazing. Queen Elizabeth

I, despite the prevailing laws against witchcraft, employed as her regular consultant the magician Dr. John Dee, whose magic stone, by means of which he claimed to divine the future, may be seen at the British Museum today.

The Reformation introduced an era of anarchy and anxiety which persisted until the middle of the seventeenth century. Superstition at this time became consolidated in the fear of witchcraft, and during the wild search for scapegoats hundreds of helpless women were sent to their deaths. Irrational terror clouded the minds of rustic heresy-hunters and monarchs alike.

It is not generally known that King Charles I was strongly influenced by fears of what fate might hold in store for him. At one period of crisis during the civil wars, he made what has been described as a "Trial of Fortune" by opening a copy of Virgil at random, and found himself reading the fatal lines:

> Oppressed with numbers in the virginal field
> His men discouraged and himself expelled.

And during his trial when the golden head of his staff became detached and fell to the ground, he thought that symbolised his own doom; he admitted to the Bishop of London that he found this a very disturbing incident.

Phantom armies were frequently seen and the ghosts of the great returned to haunt the lands where they had once ruled. Even the dead Oliver Cromwell appeared in spectral shape near where Red Lion Square in London now stands. It is not generally known that there was once a tradition that the die of the gold crowns bearing Oliver Cromwell's head became cracked across the neck after a few impressions had been struck and that this was considered so ominous that the whole issue was discontinued.

Charles II, when about to flee the kingdom, consulted an astrologer to discover the best place for safety. At the end of the century John Evelyn, on December 12th, 1680, looking out of his window, saw an omen in the shape of "a meteor of an obscure bright colour very much like the blade of a sword. . . . But such another phenomena I remember to have seen in 1640, about the trial of the great Earl of Strafford preceding our bloody revolution. . . . What this does portend, God only knows".

John Aubrey, the whimsical antiquarian, was the type of man who regarded twitchings and ticklings of the left side of his nose as having the most sinister implications. Blackstone, the eminent

English jurist upon whose teachings English law is based, believed implicitly in witches and evil spirits. Peter the Great of Russia, who lived in England for a time, had a pathological terror of walking over bridges.

The end of the Stuart line witnessed a more forthright assault upon some of the more superstitious absurdities in high places and saw King William III refusing to apply the so-called miraculous remedy of the Royal Touch for the cure of the King's evil (scrofula) while the Hanoverian line discontinued the custom altogether. It was in the reign of George II that the cruel persecution of witches was finally outlawed, signifying that among the upper classes at least the grosser superstitions were rapidly becoming outmoded. Even so, the eminent divine John Wesley continued to insist upon the execution of witches, in accordance with the teaching of Holy Writ.

The eighteenth century, which saw the decline of one type of mysticism, provided a framework for many curious expressions of the same principles in private life. Samuel Johnson always entered and left a building with his right foot foremost, since to his mind to do otherwise "brought down evil on the inmates". The unhappy Mozart was obsessed with omens. When commissioned to compose his Requiem he declared : "I am certain that I am writing a requiem for my own funeral." He was certain that it would be his last work, and so it was.

The extent to which the British triumph over the French in the Napoleonic Wars should be ascribed to supernatural agency has never been fully ascertained; nevertheless it is an undoubted fact that Nelson's flagship, the *Victory*, sailed into battle at Trafalgar reinforced by the presence of a horsehoe nailed to the mast.

The gradual elimination of superstitious practices from affairs of state did not mean that they ceased to have a potent influence so far as individual statesmen were concerned. One of the greatest victims of superstitious phobias of the nineteenth century was that child of the Age of Reason, Napoleon Bonaparte, the so-called Man of Destiny, who continually sought guidance from the clairvoyant Madame Normand and enjoyed, it was said, the companionship of a familiar sprite called "the little red man". Napoleon believed implicitly in the importance of dreams for predicting the future, and consulted a manuscript oracle known to this day as *Napoleon's Book of Fate*. He had a horror of black cats and was deeply troubled when on one occasion his horse stumbled. In view of his past efforts to keep on the right side of the spirits it must have been somewhat mortifying for him when he was offered consolation by a philosophical British Jack Tar with the comforting words: "Better luck next time", at the time when he was about to commence his exile on Elba.

The private superstitions of the British people as might be expected followed closely upon traditional lines, despite the destructive influence of industrialism and frenzied urbanisation upon old customs. The nineteenth century, however, witnessed something of a transformation in supernatural beliefs, for if magic decreased as a social force spiritualism arose to take its place. Even so, there was a good deal of superstition among the great. The doomed Abraham Lincoln observed prophetically in the midst of the American Civil War: "I feel a presentiment that I shall not outlast the rebellion. When it is over my work will be done." The Civil War had itself been heralded by curious signs and portents. There were tremendous thunderstorms, meteors were seen, and the people were awestruck at the sight of the "lurid and blood-coloured sky" which became known as "the disastrous twilight".

Here and there we are privileged to obtain a glimpse of the occult beliefs then general among the people. The assassination of Spencer Perceval, the British Prime Minister, was supposed to have been foretold in a dream, and as late as the 1860s the appearance of what was apparently a phantom sword in the heavens was hailed by the multitude as a sign of divine concern with the prevailing cholera epidemic. From the frequency of assaults on old women accused of witchcraft reported in the newspapers throughout the century, it is obvious that this age-old terror did not tend to disappear until the introduction of public education in the 1870s. As late as 1863 an Essex man was actually killed by a frenzied band of witch-hunters who believed that he had placed a spell upon a woman.

The superstitions of royalty only rarely come under public gaze, but one particular incident relating to Queen Victoria is worthy of mention. Writing from Windsor Castle in 1839 the young Queen enclosed what she described as "a little charm" which "she hopes will keep Lord Melbourne from *all evil* and which it will make her very happy if he will put it with his keys".

And in the Emerald Isles in that disturbed period John Stuart Parnell, called the uncrowned King of Ireland, was quite terrified by the colour green.

The nineteenth and early twentieth centuries witnessed an alarming situation in which one Pope and at least two monarchs were credited with having the power of the evil eye. Pope Pius IX, who died in 1898, despite his undoubted popularity among the Italian people, was generally supposed to be thus afflicted and, contrary to his obvious good intentions, was said to bring misfortune to those upon whom his eye happened to rest. It was even suggested that a blessing from His Holiness was almost the equivalent of a death sentence for the recipient. His successor, Pope Leo XIII, was also regarded with some superstitious awe because of the very high number of deaths among cardinals which occurred during his pontificate. The Emperor Napoleon III of France was also supposed to have this power and for his own protection wore a talisman on his watchguard. So also was Alphonso XIII King of Spain, whose visit to Italy in 1923 was accompanied by a series of amazing disasters involving several deaths which occurred whilst he was reviewing the Italian Fleet. There was another ominous incident in the mysterious destruction of a dam at Lake Gleno shortly after the royal train had passed by. From that time forth the King's public appearances were greeted by a furious rattling of keys—the Italian technique for keeping the forces of evil at bay.

Benito Mussolini was subject to the strangest superstitious fears and is known to have exchanged planes on one occasion after discovering that a companion on the flight, a member of his own entourage, was believed to have the evil eye. This unpleasant quality was by no means confined to dictators, kings or popes, however, and it is on record that Woodrow Wilson, the American President, was greeted by the daughter of Theodore Roosevelt with a protective gesture against the evil eye made with the fingers and known as the "mano cornuto".

Despite the advance of rationalist ideas and the retreat of the more obvious types of magical beliefs, it is clear that the great men of the twentieth century continued to be as susceptible to superstitious fears as their meanest subjects. Financiers, like all gamblers, are very susceptible to the fates, requiring constant injections of self-confidence that only the superstitious ritual can supply. The millionaire J. Pierpoint Morgan consulted astrologers, as did the American President Harding, but perhaps most amazing of all these strangely obsessed tycoons was Alfred Gwynne Vanderbilt, the American multimillionaire, who always slept with the legs of his bed standing in dishes of salt to protect himself against the attacks of evil spirits. The great J. D. Rockefeller, reputed to be the richest man in the world, carried an eagle stone in his pocket.

This was a stone found in an eagle's nest and supposed to be a charm against shipwreck and other mishaps of daily life. Whenever Rockefeller wished to confer a favour on anyone he presented him with a small piece of the ribbon by which the stone was suspended, as this was supposed to contain a very powerful type of magic and at the same time made an extremely economical gift. Winston Churchill's pleasing custom of touching passing black cats for luck was no doubt partly responsible for the final triumph of Allied arms in the Second World War, as was the gold coin carried by General Eisenhower in his pocket as a good luck charm.

Perhaps the most superstitious of all twentieth-century statesmen was Adolf Hitler, whose whole life was dominated by the need for supernatural guidance reinforced by the predictions of astrologers. Quite early in his progress he became committed to neo-paganism, a movement with dark undertones of black magic. Throughout his personal life Hitler stood in considerable awe of the number seven, despite its historic role as a symbol of Jewish mysticism. The Swastika of the Nazis was based upon a very ancient magical symbol.

The human race is apparently subject to superstitious beliefs that are obviously far too deeply rooted in the psyche to be dismissed with contempt. If such giants as Toscanini were prepared to admit that the influence of the evil eye could be held responsible for the failure of a performance at the Scala Opera House in Milan, or if, as has been claimed, an opponent of the supernatural in religion as violent as the late Italian communist leader Togliatti could carry a bent nail in his pocket as a protection against evil, then one can only admit the pressing need for some further exploration into what goes on in the human mind in times of crises. Perhaps reference should be made to the curious incident involving the late Senator Robert Kennedy shortly before his assassination. The Russian poet Yevtushenko and the American politician had drunk a toast to the prospect that Kennedy might continue his brother's work, and immediately afterwards had, in the Russian manner, thrown down the emptied goblets, which ominously failed to break. Wrote the poet : "I have always been superstitious and a terrible foreboding passed through me. I looked at Robert Kennedy. He had turned pale. Probably he, too, was superstitious."

Many of the so-called great men of history have been weaklings who sought to compensate for their inadequacies of personality by roaring like pantomime tigers and revelling at sight of the frightened faces of the more susceptible among their audiences, like some fantastic witch-doctor in his devil's mask.

Others have been strangely possessed people—thrust onwards in pursuit of a destiny that destroyed what was good and left carnage and ruin in its place. Yet others have been more modest men bearing in their hands the torch of freedom but who as often as not built up the very tyranny they loathed. All were gamblers, hosts to fortune, slaves of the ever-driving devils of inner doubt, and when physical power was threatened they, like the humblest of their subjects, turned to the most powerful god they knew—superstition.

CHAPTER XIV

THE REASON WHY

IT HAS been said that man remains a perennial prisoner of his superstitions, which hold back his progress like a ball and chain attached to his leg. Yet surely it ought to be conceded that if the basic attitudes which find expression in our superstitions have managed to survive as an integral part of personality then they must be regarded as important to the interests of the race. Superstition has been well described as "a belief or system of beliefs, based on imaginary connexions between events and incapable of being justified on rational grounds", yet this in itself prompts the question as to how mankind came to adopt its superstitions in the first place.

A vast acreage of writing has been penned on supernaturalism over the last century, for there has been a growing awareness that deeply held beliefs cannot be justly written off as mere errors of observation and reasoning, and that outward expressions are as often as not the product of what is conveniently described as the unconscious mind. However, since the basic principle underlying all human activity is the need for physical survival, one would expect to find in the more strongly entrenched traits only those factors of behaviour which the race had preserved as essential to the furtherance of this purpose.

In the foregoing pages the author has endeavoured to describe this basic struggle for survival through the agency of symbolic actions, some readily recognisable as such while others are disguised. Yet each and every superstitious action is a clearly defined protective device to offset psychic attack and to attract influences that are favourable to life. From this it will be seen that the base upon which superstitious beliefs stand four-square is that of death. Take away the fear of death, and the need for defence is rendered obsolete; given immortality the shafts of fate fall harmlessly from the armour of human imperishability. Superstition is therefore a convenient name for a process by which mankind seeks to protect itself from what is considered to be the enemy of survival.

The conflict with the spirits, being of an intangible nature, is fought out with symbols and relative concepts and the weapons are drawn from the armoury of physical experience. There is little difference in principle between the protective circle the magician employs for defence against unexpected attacks by hostile spirits and the circle of fire or the village wall which the savage builds for protection against marauding animals, while the amulet worn to intimidate the psychic foe has the same primary function as the hideous mask that is intended to undermine the morale of an enemy in battle.

Freud has pointed out in *Totem and Taboo* that primitive man came only slowly to accept death as a natural process. "The idea of death was only accepted late and with hesitancy. Even for us it has no clear content and is lacking in connotation." Fraser makes the point that disease is interpreted by savages in abstract terms, in the form of hostile attacks by invisible influences (which is not such bad thinking!). Should this be so, then we are permitted a deeper understanding into the reasons underlying contemporary superstitious beliefs. They are a necessary part of the human being's equipment for keeping alive, confirming that although we might, technologically speaking, have ceased to be savages, psychologically we remain essentially unaltered. There is no difference in principle between the bow and arrow and the hydrogen bomb; both are weapons of defence and attack, each being reserved for use against the onslaughts of a potential enemy.

Primitive man, it is said, confused "the order of thought with the order of things" and thus created the orderly yet unfruitful system we call magic. A similar fallacy could of course lie at the root of science, since its destructive power cancels out its achievements. The primary function behind each system, however, is a determination to reduce natural phenomena to a comprehensible system in order that it can be mastered, so that mankind can be made to feel relatively less insecure.

Many years ago Fraser, drawing upon the resources of his vast studies in primitive belief, published *Psyche's Task, a discourse concerning the influence of superstitions on the growth of institutions.* In this he discussed the social importance of superstitions in preserving institutions useful to society at certain stages of development, arguing that superstition, by strengthening government, has thereby contributed to the maintenance of civil order; that it has enhanced the respect for private property, and the institution of marriage; and, what is perhaps more important, has played an active part in maintaining a respect for human life, all of these factors being necessary to the growth and development of organised society.

By associating certain actions, or the neglect of such actions, with prohibitions, taboos or unhappy consequences, discipline by fear has been imposed upon society, apparently at every stage of its development. It is no doubt for this reason that the relics of superstitious usages may be found in social ceremonial today. At the same time, institutions may become outdated and cease to serve a community's need, and in this sense superstition can be a brake upon progress.

In this connection the role played by religion in supplying a protective barrier against a sense of helplessness in face of psychic attack has been of great value, for once an individual has accepted that he is protected against the evils of this life and the unthinkable terrors of death he is enabled—if only temporarily—to escape from the need for perpetual vigilance by relaxing in the arms of faith. It is for this reason that religion has always been the inveterate enemy of superstition and perhaps also why the greatest insult one religious movement can hurl against another is to accuse it of superstitious error.

In the more elaborate rites of magic, as practised by the great magicians of antiquity, we see only the more complicated and elaborate versions of what is continually being demonstrated in private superstitions. For this reason alone the priest must always remain an opponent of the magician. Yet in considering the various researches into the subject that have been made from time to time one is forced to come to the conclusion that despite scientific progress man is foredoomed to march forever in the companionship of superstition.

David Hume, in discussing the universal desire felt for the marvellous, follows this line in his *Essays* with the ponderous words : "Prodigies, omens, oracles, judgements, quite obscure the few natural events that are intermingled with them. But as the former grow thiner every page, in proportion as we advance nearer the enlightened ages ... it can never be thoroughly extirpated from human nature."

Jung believed superstition and rationalism to be complementary, which merely restates Hume's argument in more modern terms. Perhaps it is because superstition isolates a man from his community and makes him concentrate upon himself and his own selfish interest that it is able to exercise its strong fascination over the otherwise intelligent individual, reducing him to a state of mental slavery, a victim of concepts which he really knows to be false. The individual, who seeks by superstitious aids to obtain control over his own destiny, creates in effect his own personal yet immature religion, a fantasy castle in the air which affords him not the slightest protection against the very real dangers of the world in which he lives.

In posing the question as to what provides the mainspring of superstition we are left with a problem. One kind of superstition obviously arises from the conditioning process to which we are all heir—in the vast majority of cases that have been discussed we have seen how the success or otherwise of a first action of a series can determine the type of action taken in those that follow; the cricketer will retain in his pocket—sometimes for years—the lucky button which has become associated in his mind with a successful innings; and in the scientific field, B. F. Skinner, in an experiment carried out upon chickens, established that a particular bird which turned its head in a clockwise direction when first given food, repeated the action despite the fact that no further food was supplied to it. This at least suggests one rational clue as to the impulse behind the curious physical and mental rites that recur, unchangeably in both superstition and magic. Primitive man must have been aware that his sole contact with the world was by the agency of touch, sight and sound, and it is perhaps for this reason that we as superstitious individuals imagine that there is a *psychological* relationship between the toucher and the object touched. The power of the eye to embrace phenomena might also be at the root of the deeply-seated belief in the evil eye. The function of the voice as the instrument for calling another individual might be the source of the superstition that one can actually create a situation by the process of naming it; "Speak of the Devil and he is sure to appear", is a principle applicable to many spheres of activity.

All this, of course, lies in the sphere of hypothesis or, as some unkind critic might suggest, pure guesswork, but basically it does seem to indicate a continuing overvaluation of psychological acts or beliefs, a kind of omnipotence of thought which suggests to some people the possibility of assuming some control over their own environment.

The superstitions that usually find their way into the province of psychiatry belong, of course, to the area of the unquiet mind. Men and women who are subject to irrational fears will often suffer from phobias, some of which fall easily into the category of superstition. Fear of high places, of solitude, of certain hours, and even of darkness might easily be classified as evidence of disturbed mental states, but a terror of meeting cross-eyed men, which is a very common malady of this kind, is not necessarily a personal phobia but might well belong to that vast cultural heritage of mankind, the collective folklore of superstitions. At the same time the fear of tempting Providence by anticipation or by boasting could well arise out of terror of offending the father-figure, externalised as god, by trespassing upon his territory.

In assessing the situations favourable to superstitious beliefs one has to take into consideration not only the deeply felt attraction for the marvellous which is part of the human heritage, its weakness and its strength, but tricks of the mind and errors of observation and judgement which lead one into false assumptions. Stress and anxiety are conducive to hallucinatory conditions, and these play a considerable part in maintaining psychic beliefs that cannot be demonstrated scientifically; but whereas among hysterics the hallucination would have a tendency to reflect contemporary myths like the flying saucer, that of the normal individual who has been reduced to a condition of anxiety by some threatening situation which is felt to be beyond human control would tend to reflect the mythology of the culture. Into this category come witches and ghosts, and very occasionally fairies, although the latter were fast disappearing from popular mythology as long ago as the sixteenth century. Paul Bauer, in his illuminating work *Christianity or Superstition*, which is largely concerned with modern German supernaturalism, makes an interesting comment on the negative aspects of the reversion to primitive type of thought by so-called scientific man : "There is a further fundamental difference between primitive man and the superstitious man who suddenly reverts to the primitive man's world. The former was completely at home in it and was prepared to sacrifice for it and to obey its ruthless customary laws. The latter, on the other hand, makes use of magic to secure his own selfish happiness."

This is most certainly true in the case of the curious superstitious rites with which modern man surrounds himself, and which he brings into play in special situations in which he feels himself under psychic attack. It is so often the separateness and loneliness felt by the individual that creates the need for these reinforcements. The same rule applies in the case of group practices like modern witchcraft, in which lonely people attempt to create a sympathetic bond between each other by creating a highly specialised system of collective rites based upon rhythm and touch.

The problem of human gullibility ought to be given due consideration when discussing the more troublesome role of unfounded beliefs in human affairs. Curtis MacDougall discusses this aspect in great detail in his extremely interesting book *Hoaxes*, in which he points out that false beliefs can very often be ascribed to indifference, ignorance and superstition. In MacDougall's opinion superstitious man is his own worst enemy. "Indifferent, ignorant, vain, suggestible, awed by the real or feigned presence of those who speak with authority, man believes what he wants to believe." "Wants", or perhaps "needs"? It is a pressing need for the strong hand of authority which compels the individual to turn to deities, anthropomorphic and otherwise, in times of stress, in an attempt to maintain or restore the balance of the temporarily unbalanced personality. But some types of authority might well be the greatest enemy of the individual, since they could create a false sense of security in a situation which demands serious thought and positive action, playing precisely the same role as the absolutions sold by the papal authorities in the later Middle Ages, which provided for the sinner the illusion that he had purchased immunity from the terrors of hell.

The question of what type of person is likely to be inclined towards superstition has not yet been properly investigated. Superstition is often considered to be òne of the traits of the authoritarian type who needs some firmly laid down rule of procedure, the ready-made "philosopher's stone" capable of transforming an apparently unmanageable situation into one that can be managed. Gustav Yahoda, in his book *The Psychology of Superstition* refers to the frequent statement that working-class people are more liable to superstition than those of other classes. This author suggests that anxious working-class people show a greater tendency towards superstitious practices than non-anxious ones and the same principle can be applied to other classes. In fact people seem to be riddled by superstitious fears precisely in so far as they feel insecure.

The collective type·of superstition exists in every walk of life, the overt expressions varying according to class and culture. It can be taken for granted, one would suggest, that the anxious millionaire would be less likely than the labourer to touch a shovel for luck, unless of course he had made his wealth the hard way and regarded this implement as the symbol of his first success.

In every discussion on superstitions the question must arise as to whether they serve any useful purpose other than to supply a very unreliable sense of security or guide-line for the anxious. There is good reason to suppose that in some circumstances what is regarded as supernaturalism might provide an index to very real states and conditions. A dream or an auditory hallucination could well draw attention to the existence of an illness, the milder symptoms of which the sufferer refuses to acknowledge. In both psychology and superstition stumbling is a fairly conclusive sign that one is emotionally ill-equipped to carry out a particular action at a particular time.

Freud has pointed out in his *Totem and Taboo* that the super-stitious horror of blood found both in savage communities and among the supposedly civilised possibly "serves aesthetic and hygienic purposes which are obliged in every case to cloak themselves behind magical motives". In treating of the universal superstitious taboo against leaving a knife with the edge upwards he says : "May we not recognise in this taboo a premonitory warning against possible 'symptomatic acts' in the execution of which a sharp weapon might be employed by unconsciously evil impulses." Knocking on wood, it would appear, might well be a useful process by providing a physical outlet for the immediate reduction of tension. Possibly the most com-monly found superstition of all, and one which is supposed to have a useful function is the conviction that to disregard the "inner voice" that offers counsel in favour of one particular course of action or warns against another, is to make oneself the accomplice of one's own downfall. Time and time again one comes upon a profound belief in an "inner consciousness" which in contemporary life seems to have replaced the protective spirit or guardian angel of earlier faiths.

Even in the mundane field of good and bad luck there is a strong possibility that human attitudes can have some influence on our affairs. Some psychologists contend that a man who believes himself to be unlucky in business may be in reality no more than a poor listener, more concerned with what he intends to say himself than with the opening of his mind to impressions from outside which success demands. In matters of chance the subject becomes much more complicated. The professional gambler in realms of pure chance like dice-throwing, in which there are thirty-six different ways for the dice to fall, has the advantage of knowing that the risks can be calculated exactly. In some types of gambling, however, there are non-mathematical factors to be taken into consideration, a typical example being horse-racing, which involves the study of form and an intent listening for the whisperings of fate from the direction of the stable. It has even been suggested that there are circumstances in which making a random decision on the basis of the turn of a wheel or the tossing of a coin might be more conducive to success than relying upon experience or knowledge, which may be inadequate or based upon false premises.

Superstitions are part of the idiom of the people and may therefore be expected to vary in the same way that dialect varies, whilst still maintaining the basic characteristics which distinguish one type of belief from another. The minor variations are immaterial, however, the repetition of a constant theme being the real index to the power of a particular superstition within a community. The mechanics of superstition are indications of a type of mystical thinking that is found more often among primitives than among scientifically orientated modern man. Superstition belongs to a dream world where thoughts are things, where time often has another meaning and cause and effect are relatively unexplored concepts. There is no second hand ticking away in nature's clock and likewise there is no immutable order of progress in abstract concepts. Yesterday may be another today, tomorrow may be yesterday. To the magician, past, present and future appear as an unbroken panorama. Our supernaturalisms belong to the irrational side of our nature, but the savage who observes the rules of superstition does at least attempt to regulate life by what he imagines to be the laws of cause and effect, and to this extent superstitions can serve a rational need; it is often better to follow the rule of superstition than to be without any rule of life at all.

In surveying the whole scene of the supernatural it is perhaps legitimate to suggest that, since mankind as a whole is incapable of seeing beyond what is possible, the arts of prophecy, clairvoyance and the power of magic, even if they have not worked in the past, might yet be made to function in that other dimension—science—at some time in the future. In this sense we may see in the magic carpet the antecedent of the hovercraft. If scientists were not so bigoted, so fearful of admitting in public what in private conversation they will almost invariably concede to be possible, we might yet see the day when the physical side of life became united with the spiritual aspect from which it has apparently been slipping away since man gave up living among the apes.

To conclude on a somewhat sombre note, it is obvious that given that the struggle for survival lies at the root of all human activity, then death, the unmentionable enemy with which man struggles in vain to come to terms, must be the prime denominator underlying all our apprehensions. Take away death and there is no fear, nor is there doubt, which is the child of uncertainty, nor any devils or the need for gods to counter-balance them. If the fear of death were to vanish from the earth we would achieve an existence free of the terrors of psychic attack and of the need for psychic defence; but alas, when life has been robbed of its dark, menacing threat of sorrow, hope, the hand-maid of superstition, will likewise have vanished from the earth.

BIBLIOGRAPHY

Arnold, Thurman, W., *The Folklore of Capitalism*, Yale University Press, 1937.

Barker, J. C., M.D., *Scared to death, An examination of fear, its cause and effects*, Muller, 1968.

Bauer, Paul, *Christianity or Superstition*, Marshall Morgan and Scott, 1966

Bonaparte, Marie, *Myths of War*, Imago Publishing Co., 1947.

Brelsford, Vernon, *Superstitious Survivals*, Centaur Press, London 1958.

Debrunner, H., *Witchcraft in Ghana*, Presbyterian Book Depot, Kumasi 1957.

Elworthy, F. T., *The Evil Eye*, The Julian Press Inc., N.Y. 1958.

Flugel, J. C., *Man, Morals and Society*, Peregrine Edition, 1962.

Forman, Henry J , *The Story of Prophecy*, Cassell and Co., 1936.

Frazer, Sir J. G., *Psyche's Task*, Dawsons Pall Mall, 1968.

Freud, Sigmund, *Totem and Taboo*, Routledge and Kegan Paul, 1950.

Gifford, Edward S., *The Charms of Love*, Faber and Faber, 1962.

Hole, Christina (Editor), *Encyclopaedia of Superstition*, Hutchinson, 1961.

Howard, Alexander, *Endless Cavalcade—A Diary of British Festivals and Customs*, Arthur Barker, 1964.

Jahoda, Gustav, *The Psychology of Superstition*, Allen Lane, The Penguin Press, 1969.

Jastrow, Joseph, *Error and Eccentricity in Human Belief*, Dover Publications Inc., N.Y. 1962.

Krappe, Alexander H., *The Science of Folk-lore*, Methuen, 1962

Leland, Charles G., *Etruscan Magic and Occult Remedies*, University Books, N.Y. 1963.

Lewinsohn, Richard, *Prophets and Prediction*, Secker, 1961.

Maple, Eric, *Magic, Medicine and Quackery*, Robert Hale, 1968.

Maudsley, Henry, *Natural Causes and Supernatural Seemings*, Kegan Paul Trench & Co.,1886.

Middleton, John, *Magic Witchcraft and Curing*, National History Press, New York 1967.

Opie, Iona and Peter, *The Lore and Language of Schoolchildren*, Oxford Univ. Press, 1967.

Rawcliffe, D. H., *Illusions and Delusions of Supernatural and Occult*, Dover Books, 1959

Rycroft, Charles, *Anxiety and Neurosis*, Allen Lane, The Penguin Press, 1968.

Sargant, W., *The Battle for the Mind*, Heinemann, 1957.

Skinner, Charles, *Myths and Legends of Flowers, Trees, Fruits and Plants*, J. B. Lippincott (USA,)1925.

Spence, Lewis, *Myth and Ritual in Dance Games and Rhyme*, Watts, 1947.

Thiselton-Dyer, T. F., *Folk-lore of Women*, Elliot Stock, 1905.

Thompson, C. J. S., *The Hand of Destiny*, Rider, London 1932.